A NEW ILLUSTRATED HISTORY OF THE

NAZIS

A NEW ILLUSTRATED HISTORY OF THE NAZIS

D&C
David and Charles

Project Editor: Flavio Fiorani
Author: Alessandra Minerbi
English translation from the Italian text: Donald Bathgate and Brenda Porster for NTL, Florence
Graphics: Enrico Albisetti
Page layout: Giovanni Bartoli
Maps: Sergio Biagi Comunicazione Grafica

A DAVID & CHARLES BOOK
David & Charles is a subsidiary of F+W (UK) Ltd.,
an F+W Publications Inc. company

First published in the UK in 2005
Originally published in Italy in 2002 © Giunti Editore S.p.A., Florence–Milan
Original Title: Storia Illustrata del Nazismo

Distributed in North America
by F+W Publications, Inc.
4700 East Galbraith Road
Cincinnati, OH 45236
1-800-289-0963

A catalogue record for this book is available from the British Library.

ISBN 0 7153 2101 3

Printed in Italy by Giunti Industrie Grafiche S.p.A., Prato
for David & Charles
Brunel House Newton Abbot Devon

Visit our website at www.davidandcharles.co.uk

David & Charles books are available from all good bookshops; alternatively you can contact our Orderline on (0)1626 334555 or write to us at FREEPOST EX2 110, David & Charles Direct, Newton Abbot, TQ12 4ZZ (no stamp required UK mainland).

Contents

A NEW ILLUSTRATED HISTORY OF THE NAZIS

The establishment of the Weimar Republic

During the course of the first decade of the twentieth century, the international balance of power became increasingly precarious due to growing rivalries, especially between Germany on the one hand and France and Great Britain on the other. The Balkans constituted one of the most dangerous breeding grounds of tension, and the assassination of the heir to the Austrian throne at the hands of Serbian nationalists in Sarajevo on 28 June 1914 led to the explosion of a conflict that saw two sides opposed to one another: Austria and Germany on one side and Great Britain, France and Russia on the other.

The German ruling class was determined to go to war both to strengthen its own power and to try and enact its expansionist

Solar Eclipse (1926)
In George Grosz's painting, soldiers, capitalists and headless men sit round a table – a metaphor for defeat and for a Germany prostrated by economic crisis. (Page 8)

Steel Helmets
Association of fighting men's parade against the Versailles Treaty. (Page 9)

German War Wounded and Prisoners
(Below and right)

policies in continental Europe. In 1914, the General Staff of the German army was convinced that the conflict would be short-lived. However, after a number of hard-fought victories, it was clear that this was going to be a case of trench warfare, based on reciprocal attrition and conditioned by the economic power of the countries involved. The long battle fought at Verdun against the French (February–September 1916) did not bring about the hoped-for turning point, but it did lead to significant political changes. Well aware that his role was becoming less and less important, Emperor Wilhelm II entrusted supreme command of the army to Marshal Paul von Hindenburg and to his Chief of Staff Erich Ludendroff, thereby creating the conditions for a genuine military dictatorship. The policies followed by the new leaders were aimed on the one hand at intensifying the military build-up in order to make maximum use of available resources, and on the other to employ the most audacious means possible in the conduct of the war, especially by boosting submarine warfare. During 1917, the military state of the Reich was becoming more and more precarious. In addition, foodstuffs were becoming increasingly scarce and a general weariness was making itself felt both among front-line soldiers and the civilian population, all of which contributed to heightening class tensions. The example of Russia, where peace and a new, revolutionary order had been established at the price of social unrest, was increasingly being echoed in Germany, where the population was by now near to exhaustion.

The General Staff was still hoping to reach a compromise peace agreement. Instead, unconditional surrender became inevitable through the growing involvement of the United States, the decline of Austria and above all the collapse of the domestic front. To prevent the disintegration of the country, the government, presided over by the Chancellor, Prince Max of Baden, tried to convince the Kaiser to abdicate in order

Quelling Protesters in Berlin
Soldiers positioned on a rooftop about to open fire in January 1919.

The Big City (1927)
Otto Dix's painting shows an old soldier on crutches. (Below)

to save the monarchy, and carried out a political reform, the cornerstones of which were universal suffrage and the attribution of full legislative powers to parliament. But by now discontent was too widespread, and when at the end of October sailors staged a mutiny at the port of Kiel, the protest spread to many other industrial centres, to Berlin and to the troops on duty at the Franco-Belgian front. The Kaiser was forced to flee to Holland.

The Birth of the Republic

After the abdication of the Kaiser, the Chancellor convinced Friedrich Ebert, head of the German Social-Democratic Party (SPD), to form a government. But the SPD had no long-term political aim and was unequipped to deal with the pace of events. The republic, proclaimed in Berlin on 9 November 1918, had been forced into being by rioting crowds. This institutional break with the past marked the culmination of the long dissolution of the German Empire to which the war had dealt the *coup de grace*. The SPD, who were the reluctant champions of this radical process of change, tried to curb the extremist tendencies that were espoused by the movement of the 'people's councils', whose main centres were located in Berlin and Bavaria. However, the new government felt obliged to seek the support of the reactionary monarchical General Staff and the 'free corps' made up of nationalists, who were given *carte blanche* to act against the revolutionary left. In January, an attempted insurrection by the Communist Party was quelled. A month later, Kurt Eisner, President of the Bavarian People's Council Republic, was assassinated.

It was clear that the Social Democrats were incapable of dealing with the demands of the radical wing of the German workers' movement – who had been fired by the October Revolution in Russia and

Ernst von Salomon

Born in 1902, Ernst von Salomon was the son of a Prussian officer who later became head of the Frankfurt criminal police force. He was one of the most important figures of the generation, whose first-hand experience of the war led to a spirit of rebellion against both the old imperial order and the new democratic one, which many considered incapable of guiding the rebirth of the German people and restoring the nation to its role as a great power. Von Salomon was a militant member of the "free corps" and was active against the Spartacists in Berlin. In 1920, he took part in the Wolfgang Kapp Putsch and in 1922 was involved in the assassination of Walther Rathenau, the Foreign Minister. Von Salomon was arrested and sentenced to five years imprisonment; after his release he dedicated himself to publishing and to political journalism. His autobiography, *I Proscritti,* was published in 1930. More than any other work of the time, this book bears witness to the mixture of rebelliousness and activism that characterized his generation. 'It wasn't important that what we did seemed to be right; what was important in those suffocating days was to act. The future of Germany was by now in the hands of single individuals, and in that incomparable moment of grace every individual had a direct part to play in German destiny.' Arrested by the Americans in 1945, he was interned until the following year, after which he dedicated himself to political journalism. He died in 1972.

KARL LIEBKNECHT
Pacifist, and the founder of the Spartacus League and the German Communist Party, who was assassinated in Berlin in January 1919.

RED STAR
The official organ of the German Communists. The party abandoned the idea of revolutionary uprisings and made major inroads in the 1920s among the working classes who had been hard hit by the economic crisis.

the two-year period of Communist popularity that followed all over Europe – without the support of the old order. The elections for the Constituent Assembly in January 1919 – the first with universal voting rights – rewarded the Republican Coalition (Social Democrats, Democrats and Catholics) and registered a clear defeat for both the conservatives and the extreme left. But the harsh clauses of the peace treaty imposed by the Triple Entente made the job of the parties that constituted the 'Weimar Coalition' even more difficult. At the first political elections in June 1920, the trend was clearly reversed: the coalition's share of the vote fell from 73 per cent to 43.6 per cent and there was increasing support for the more radical parties both on the right and on the left. There then began a long period of minority government rule that was forced to lean on the support of either the Social Democrats or the conservatives as the occasion required.

THE PEACE TREATY AND THE 'STAB IN THE BACK'

The postwar peace conference opened in Paris in May 1919. The representatives of the victorious powers were convinced that the responsibility for World War I was Germany's alone and that the best way to neutralize this dangerous nation was to weaken it economically, politically and militarily.

The Treaty of Versailles, which imposed the victors' conditions on the defeated Reich, was signed on 28 June 1919. Germany lost 13 per cent of its territory, including industrial land with 75 per cent of the country's iron-ore deposits and 25 per cent of its coal mines. Alsace and Lorraine were returned to the French, who had ceded these territories to Germany in 1870, and an area of Prussia became part of the newly founded Poland. The German colonies were divided into 'mandates' (in effect equivalent to colonial domains) and were shared between France and Great Britain, and Belgium, Japan

ROSA LUXEMBURG

Born in Poland in 1871, Rosa Luxemburg studied in Zurich where she came into contact with the leaders of the Polish Social Democrat movement. In the years following her move to Berlin in 1898, she became one of the most lucid and dedicated theoreticians of the socialist movement. At the outbreak of World War I, she denounced the policy of loyalty to the fatherland espoused by the German Social Democrats and played a key role in the birth of the Spartacist movement. Despite being in favour of the Bolshevik revolution, she was able to point to the dangers inherent in the Soviet political regime. After the founding of the Weimar Republic, she was a fierce critic of the Social Democrats' moderation and readiness to compromise, feeling that only a radical break with the past would make it possible to create the foundations for a truly democratic renewal of Germany. She was a founding member of the German Communist Party, in favour of participating in the elections for the Constituting Assembly and opposing any suggestion of an insurrection. During the Berlin riots in 1919 – which could be seen as episodes of a genuine civil war – she was assassinated, along with Karl Liebknecht. Her death was soon followed by the repression of the movement of soldiers' and workers' councils in Bavaria. These two episodes marked a further step in the rehabilitation of the military forces of the old order, confirming the tendency of the republic to choose an alliance with the right wing in order to put down the forces of revolution.

ELECT SPARTACUS
The Communist fist comes down hard on the fragile Weimar parliamentary democracy.

SPARTACISTS STREET-FIGHTING IN THE CAPITAL
(Below)

PRISONER ERNST TOLLER
The German playwright portrayed during his imprisonment. (Bottom)

and Australia. The reparations that Germany would have to pay within 30 years amounted to 132 thousand million gold marks.

Thanks mainly to the commitment of the American President Woodrow Wilson, the League of Nations was formed, with its headquarters in Geneva. This was to be an organ of permanent mediation and arbitration for the peaceful resolution of international conflicts. However, Germany was not admitted, providing yet further confirmation of the desire to punish Germany, and also reflecting the fragile nature of the group since one of the most important European nations had been excluded. The harshness of the conditions imposed on Germany unleashed discontent among large swathes of the population, and the new democratic government was given the blame for a situation that was created by defeat in the war. The inevitable effect of defeat was the humiliation of a nation whose identity, before and during the war, was based on military strength. There was a widespread feeling that it was the new leaders who were responsible for 'the stab in the back'; they were accused of adopting defeatist policies and of being incapable of defending Germany's honour at the negotiating table.

ERNST TOLLER

Born in 1893 of a well-to-do Jewish family, Ernst Toller enrolled as a volunteer in the war and converted to pacifism during the conflict. In 1918, he joined the revolutionary left and took part in the short-lived Bavarian Councils' Republic, becoming its president following the assassination of Kurt Eisner. After the downfall of the government, he was sentenced to five years imprisonment. During the course of the revolution, Toller affirmed his belief in a 'revolution of love', and after its failure he took his leave of the extreme left, declaring the need for social conflicts to be resolved by non-violent means. Upon his release from prison he continued to take part in the pacifist movement and was among those on the left who did not support either Communist extremism or socialist moderation. During the Weimar years, he wrote the important works that were to make him one of the most disturbing leaders of the expressionist theatre. In 1933, he went into exile in the United States, where he contributed to numerous periodicals published by emigrants. He committed suicide in 1939 when he heard the news of the takeover of Madrid by Franco's troops. Among his most important works were *Masse Mensch* (1921; *Masses and Man*), about contrasts within the German left; *Hoppla; Wir Leben!* (1927; *Such is Life*), about the meanness of spirit of the Weimar Republic; and finally the autobiographical *Eine Jugend in Deutschland* (1933; *I was a German*), which traces the tragic destiny of the German-Jewish bourgeoisie.

STEEL HELMETS
Hindenburg was honorary president of the paramilitary organization during the 1920s.

NSDAP POSTER FOR THE 1930 ELECTIONS
(Below)

THE BIRTH OF THE NSDAP

The first nucleus of the Nazi Party was founded in Munich in 1919, and the following year it took the name of the National German Socialist Workers' Party (NSDAP). In 1920, its programme was made public, even though the most characteristic feature of the new movement was its uncontrolled activism, far more important than any theoretical programme. It soon evolved into a paramilitary group; the majority of its members came from the 'free corps' and from the *Reichswehr* and their purpose was to carry on the struggle against the Weimar government with no respect to the rules of democratic process. Combat units known as the SA were formed to provide a street-fighting arm of the NSDAP. From the end of 1920, the daily *Volkischer Beobachter* began to appear, financed by the *Reichswehr* and by private parties. Adolf Hitler took over as leader of the party in 1921, and personalities such as Alfred Rosenberg, Rudolf Hess and Hans Frank – all destined to play a fundamental role in the future of Germany – started to become increasingly active. In January 1923, the first party congress was held, with 20,000 members attending. Even if it was still mostly Bavarian-based, the NSDAP had grown considerably, and it had no aims to become a party that, like all the others, only looked after its own interests in the parliamentary arena.

A march on Rome by Fascists in October 1922, and the victory of the movement in Italy, had a galvanizing effect on the National Socialists, even though they drew their strength mainly from the situation in Germany, from the climate of exasperated nationalism and from the social protest caused by the difficult postwar situation. The NSDAP had grown in appeal due to factors such as Germany's rising inflation and the serious crisis of confidence that had affected the middle and lower middle classes, who were unwilling to unite with the proletariat in a common battle for social rights.

THE NSDAP PROGRAMME

The very first Nazi Party programme was drawn up in 1920. Hitler always maintained that it was important not to be tied to an inflexible project, and the programme was conceived essentially as a propaganda instrument, although it already contained the basis for much of the political activity that would take place in the years to come. The points of the programme included dismantling the Versailles conditions and creating a Greater Germany to re-establish borders and to give land to a growing population. Much room was given over to attacks against the plurality of parties and the parliamentary system, which were contrasted with a national community that would make political parties not only useless, but also harmful. It was also stated – and this was to become a fixed cornerstone of Nazi propaganda – that only citizens of German blood could make up this national community; everyone else, above all the Jews, could only live in Germany as guests. It is clear, therefore, that in 1920 the party was already a racist and anti-Semitic movement. The most demagogic aspects of the programme were the request for a high degree of state control and the struggle against so-called 'interest slavery' that is, the elimination of the speculation characteristic of the capitalist system. However, the increasingly close alliance it formed with the major industrial and financial interests led the NSDAP to abandon this position towards the end of the 1920s.

THE WEIMAR CONSTITUTION

The constitution signed at Weimar in 1919 represented one of the most advanced documents of its kind at the time. Liberal in inspiration, it was the result of a compromise with two other democratic forces, the socialists and the Catholics. While the two socialist parties had single objectives as regards constitutional policy, they lacked the overall picture. In recognition of the liberals' greater experience in these matters, they left the responsibility of drafting the charter of government to Hugo Preuss, the new Secretary of State. The Weimar Constitution outlined a system whereby executive power was linked to the coalitions formed in parliament. A special role fell to the President of the Republic, elected by universal suffrage and who, according to article 48, could govern by presidential ordinance in an emergency. He therefore played a fundamental role as an alternative to the power of parliament. The law that was to have defined, as far as was possible, what constituted such an emergency was never passed, and so it was left vague and therefore open to differing judgments. The legislative power of the Reichstag (parliament) was also limited by the introduction of the referendum. As far as the organization of society was concerned, the constitution did not decide between capitalism and socialism, limiting itself to a minimal consensus: the basis of future legislation was to be the existing order, founded on private property, but it was to be adapted in a social sense and, if the necessary majority was reached in the legislature, it could be given a more sociaist slant. This, however, never happened in the years that followed. The economy was to be run on a solidarity-oriented basis: article 165 stated the principle of parity between capital and labour, and assured state recognition to both partners of collective contracts and to their agreements. On this point, the text of the constitution was more explicit than on almost all the other points of economic and social matters. The provisions for socialization did not go beyond those contained in the 'Socialization Law' of March 1919. The part directly inspired by social-democratic ideas gave broad recognition to civil rights and outlined the framework for a welfare state. After lengthy negotiations and many compromises, the constitution was approved on 31 July 1919, with 262 pros against 75 cons.

The Victory of Republican Thought
Political cartoon by George Grosz.

Young German Women
Cooking lessons for future housewives.

From stability to crisis

The years between the end of the period of hyper-inflation (1923) and the Great Depression (1929) were politically relatively stable, even though Germany was ruled by minority governments that had to rely on the goodwill of either the Social Democratic or the National Popular parties as the need arose. These were years of economic recovery, during which Germany made its return to international politics, and of less social unrest. However, it was in this period that the contradictions and limitations of the Weimar Republic came to the fore, the same contradictions and limitations that were to explode in the forthcoming decade. In April of 1925, the first presidential elections held under universal suffrage took place. Thanks to the support of the nationalists, the military and the pan-Germanists, Marshal Paul von Hindenburg, the World War I hero, managed to defeat the Catholic candidate of the governing coalition by a margin of only a few hundred votes.

Nationalist Parade
(Page 16)

Queuing to Get into a Bank
(Page 17)

Walter Rathenau
The former president of the AEG colossus was in charge of Weimar foreign policy and negotiated cuts in reparations.

Hyperinflation
Bank note for 100 billion marks.

Distributing Food (Below)

This result marked a crucial point in the decline that the republic had been undergoing since its inception. The problem was the limited nature in which it implemented democracy, which it only saw fit to introduce at parliamentary level, thus ruling out grass-roots participation in other areas. Nor could the young republic count on fresh state apparatus that would be wholly faithful to the underlying tenets of democracy. The parliamentary elections held in 1928 gave a clear warning signal: the Social Democrat and Communist parties emerged as victors, while the parties of the centre were defeated. The votes that were lost by the forces that had until then formed the governments of the republic went to various local groups. This fragmentation was symptomatic of the inability of the bourgeois parties to win over the centre of the political spectrum. Besides this, the Communists and the Socialists held conflicting positions; divided as they were by irreconcilable contrasts, they refused to form an alliance in a common battle against the right-wing forces, the first to benefit from Germany's growing political instability.

Reparations and Inflation

The reparations imposed on Germany were so high that it was impossible to rebuild the devastated economy of a country exhausted by the war effort. The question of payment was one of the central issues of German politics and became one of the prime causes of government instability and of ideological agitation by extremist forces both on the right and the left. Walter Rathenau, Minister of Reconstruction and of Foreign Affairs (1921–22), was among those who were most active in the attempt to solve this complicated situation. He

ONE ROOM FOR A FAMILY WITH SIX CHILDREN
The conditions imposed by the peace treaty had catastrophic consequences on the country's economy: unemployment and poverty not only crushed Germany's poorest classes but its urban middle classes, too. (Below)

was convinced of the need to satisfy the demands of the victorious powers, but was also aware that the impoverished German economy made it impossible to meet them completely.

The extremely high sums being paid in reparations, social welfare spending, the cost of supporting war widows and orphans, and the enormous minting of paper money that had served to finance the war in Germany as in other countries, all served to ignite an inflation that flared out of control. The exchange rate was 4.2 marks to the dollar at the start of the war; by January 1929 it had grown to 64.8 marks, and in 1922 it jumped to 17,972 marks. In 1923, inflation reached its peak, reducing a huge proportion of the national wealth to worthlessness. The hardest hit were fixed-income sectors like the working and middle classes and creditors, particularly the banks. On the other hand, many industrialists profited from the situation, using credit granted at easy terms to finance higher investments and form large conglomerations. Farmers and mortgage-holders were also favoured because they could repay their debt in a devalued currency. Measures implemented by the Minister of the Economy, Hans Luther, produced the monetary reform that eventually brought about the end of the emergency in 1923. The most serious economic problems had by then been overcome, but the years of great inflation left a lasting sense of insecurity and a lack of trust in the state.

ECONOMIC RECOVERY, INDUSTRY AND AGRICULTURE

The difficulties linked to the excessively high reparations were clear. The United States, which generously financed the economic recovery of many European countries in the years following the war, was convinced of the importance of not

LITVINOV AND RATHENAU
The Soviet Foreign Minister (left) and his German counterpart (centre) signed the Treaty of Rapallo in April 1922, launching economic cooperation between the two nations.

SABOTAGE IN THE RUHR
French locomotive put out of action by German railway workers. (Below)

allowing Germany's economy to be totally suffocated. In 1924, the American banker and politician, Charles Dawes, devised a plan to encourage Germany's recovery through cutting reparations by splitting them into annual instalments. Besides this, a group of American banks granted the country a loan of 800 million marks. With the Dawes Plan, the flow of American credit started up again, and the German economy entered a phase of restructuring and rationalization. In 1927, Germany regained the same levels of production as it had prior to the war, and began importing and exporting once again. Trends that had existed at the beginning of the century were accentuated: the growth of big business and the creation of cartels; the introduction of modern methods of business management; rationalization of production; and the ever-growing presence of the state in the economy. During the 1920s, the most important areas of production – chemicals, steel, electricity and mining – concluded their cartel agreements.

Agriculture, on the other hand, was going through more serious difficulties, the roots of which were in the distant past. Its interests increasingly diverged from those of industry: by now, the power bloc between agriculture and large-scale industry that had produced Bismarck's Germany had come to an end. In the postwar years, many small farms went bankrupt, while major landowners, especially those east of the River Elbe holding vast estates with a low productivity, remained unaffected by the change. Indeed, by neglecting agrarian reform, the Weimar government unwittingly made a serious mistake that led to continuity in the power of the Second Reich. By and large, agriculture remained hostile to the republic and was one of the areas where discontent found increasingly fertile ground, especially after President Hindenburg was elected in 1925; with the economic crisis of 1929, it became a crucial force in the Nazi drive to power.

THE OCCUPATION OF THE RUHR

At the end of 1922, France took advantage of the late delivery of some German goods due as part of reparations to invade the Ruhr area. Officially, this was to guarantee 'pledged productivity'; in reality, it was done to cut off the Rhineland and the Ruhr from the Reich. The response was a wave of nationalistic uprisings exploited by the German government, and the proclamation of 'passive resistance'. The population of the region was called on to refuse to collaborate with the occupying forces. When a general strike was called, the central government shouldered the burden of paying wages and salaries. In the summer of 1923, the failure of this strategy was on the horizon – inflation was growing at dizzying rates, while the Ruhr region was prostrate. That autumn, the broad coalition formed and guided by Gustav Stresemann attempted to change direction: there was no alternative but to surrender to France. However, in the months that followed, French victory turned into German success, made possible mainly because the opponents ran out of strength. The new economic strategy and the acceptance of the Dawes Plan assured the solvency of payments. At this juncture, it was the politics of Paris that suffered. Pressed by its allies, France was forced to announce its withdrawal from the Ruhr territory in the summer of 1925. Thus the trial of strength of World War I came to an end, paving the way for a search for stability on both sides.

THE MUNICH PUTSCH

IN THE BEGINNING THERE WAS THE WORD
Hitler portrayed as a Messiah.

Nineteen twenty-three was a turning point for the NSDAP. The collapse of the mark and the explosion of nationalism that followed the occupation of the Ruhr led to the conviction that the time was ripe to attack the democratic regime in place in Germany. On the evening of 8 November, Adolf Hitler, leader of the Nazi Party, tried to take power in Bavaria, and from there, imitating Mussolini's march on Rome, intended to march on Berlin to conquer the Reich. The coup was a failure because the conservatives in Berlin mistrusted Hitler, but, as the trial against the rebels revealed, the circumstances that made the attempt possible showed how wide-reaching was the complicity enjoyed by the NSDAP in its ambition to overthrow the democratic system. The trial itself was an important opportunity to show just how fragile the republic was; although Hitler was sentenced to five years imprisonment, he managed to cut a better figure than his allies, and his attack against democracy was justified as being a demonstration of patriotism. Released after serving only one year, he was by then convinced of the need to change tactics – not a violent overthrow of power, but a gradual conquest of it by legal means.

SUPPORTERS OF THE NEWBORN NAZI PARTY

'WE'RE FOR ADOLF HITLER!'
The NSDAP sought support from the workers from the very beginning.

'WORK AND BREAD'
The Nazi promise to the electorate.

ELECTIONEERING SLOGANS
From left to right: Propaganda of the Social Democrats pointing to the danger of the Nazis; danger of the Communists (to break with the system); and the People's Party's struggle against inflation and civil war. (Below)

WORK AND TRADE UNIONS

The bargaining power of the workers, and particularly of organized trade unions, grew significantly during the Weimar years. The war had irrevocably sanctioned the importance of the productive role of the working class, and in the years following the war it was not possible for Germany to turn back. On 15 November 1918, an agreement was signed that gave birth to the Joint Central Committee for Trade Union-Industry Cooperation, thereby creating the first institutional framework for dialogue with the unions. The introduction of the eight-hour working day showed the employers' readiness to make a number of real concessions above and beyond what legislation had provided for. The economic basis for this policy of cooperation was inflation. After currency stabilization put a limit on the margin of inflationary manoeuvres available, the social foundations of the committee ceased to exist and wage disputes grew more heated as employers tried to make workers bear the brunt of price pressures by extending their working day to beyond eight hours. All prospects of cooperation faded when faced with the hard reality of class conflict. There were great divergences in how factory owners tackled this new reality; by and large, the more modern industries tended towards greater cooperation.

Between 1924 and 1928, scope for a negotiated settlement grew ever slimmer. Business wanted to get back to unlimited freedom of action, doing away with all the guarantees and provisions of the welfare state. When the economic crunch did come, the conflict exploded in all its virulence, because by then what was at stake was the democratic social system itself. Labour was increasingly torn apart by the deep-seated split between organized workers determined to protect their privileges and the growing unemployed masses.

GUSTAV STRESEMANN
One of the founder members of the People's Party, Stresemann was Chancellor for a short period at the head of a broad-based coalition. He later became the Minister of Foreign Affairs and, until 1929, was conciliatory towards France.
He won the 1928 Nobel Peace Prize.

DEMONSTRATIONS AGAINST THE VERSAILLES TREATY (Below)

THE 'SPIRIT OF LOCARNO'

The victorious powers, with France in the forefront, had not only burdened a defeated Germany with huge costs, but had also attempted to deprive it of any say in international affairs, keeping Germany out of the League of Nations and attempting to isolate the country. Gustav Stresemann, Germany's Foreign Minister from 1923 to 1929, played a leading part in finding a way out of this situation. The first major step in this direction came when a treaty of friendship with the Soviet Union was signed in Rapallo, leading to significant economic benefits thanks to the trade openings it brought in its wake.

In the years that followed, once the inflation emergency had ended and, from January 1925, the country had regained full freedom of trade, Germany began to play an increasingly significant role on the international stage. Stresemann was convinced that Europe could only find a balance of power if his own country was allowed out of isolation, and in the mid-1920s this position was shared by Great Britain and by France, in particular by Aristide Briand, French Foreign Minister from 1925 to 1932. At the Locarno Conference of October 1925, the European nations, including Germany, guaranteed mutual respect for each other's national frontiers and renounced the use of force to resolve any future disputes. The following year, Germany gained admittance to the League of Nations. In 1926, Stresemann signed a new pact declaring neutrality and friendship with the Soviet Union, showing that German foreign policy had now regained full autonomy. Many conservative Germans were critical of the excessive concessions granted to the very powers that had underwritten the harsh terms of the defeat, and they did not feel Stresemann's foreign policy could return Germany to its role as the key

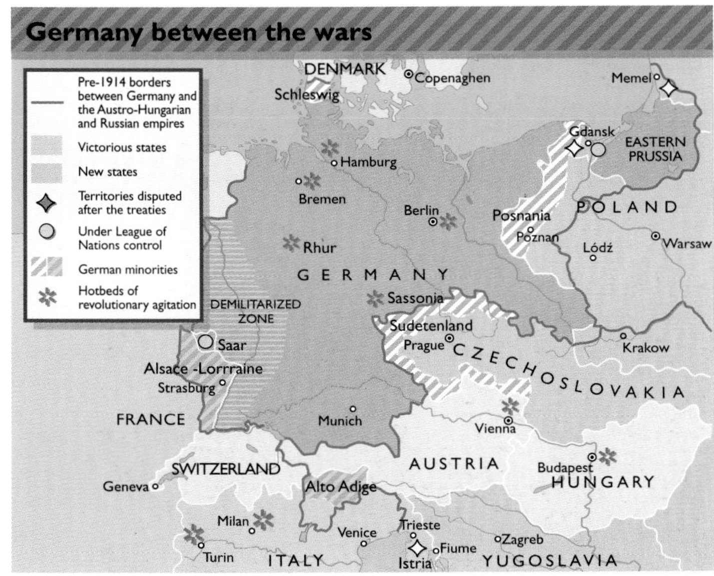

WALTER GROPIUS
Architect, designer and urban planner, Gropius was one of the leaders of the new functionalist architecture movement and the Bauhaus school of Weimar for which he designed the building in Dessau. (Below)

TRAMA NERA (1922)
A supporter of an anti-naturalistic concept of art, the Russian painter Kandinskij, who had moved to Germany at the end of the 19th century, was a master of the abstract movement. (Far right)

player in central Europe. In 1927, Stresemann and Briand received the Nobel Peace Prize; many Europeans were convinced that peace was now guaranteed for many years to come.

CULTURAL LIFE

After 1918, German cultural life was in many ways contradictory. Despite some ambitious advances in teaching methods, the school system remained unchanged both as regards curriculum and its overall organization. The majority of teachers never wholeheartedly embraced the cause of the republic, and indeed more often showed sympathy for anti-democratic ideas. However, in the realm of artistic activity, Weimar Germany experienced a season that was rich in cultural innovation, and many earlier trends could now be expressed more freely. The development of the means of mass communication found a natural audience in an ever larger and more varied public. Literature and theatre discovered new forms, from the spread of reportage as a literary genre, to the important experience of the political theatre of Erwin Piscator, to cabaret.

Mass production of items for use in the home led to the changeover of the applied arts from crafts to industry. The birth of the Bauhaus as a formative cultural centre committed to the renovation of home architecture and furnishings brought together, first in Weimar and then in Dessau, architects (Walter Gropius), painters (Oskar Schlemmer, Vassilij Kandinskij, Johannes Itten) and photographers (Lazló Moholy-Nagy, John Heartfield). In opposition to what was seen as the 'decadent' bourgeois love of embellishment were born the 'new objectivity' movement and expressionism, both of which saw themselves as genuine interpreters of daily life, close to the common people. Against decorative and catalogued styles in architecture, building was free of ornament, becoming immediate and direct.

MASS SOCIETY AND LEISURE TIME

During the 1920s, Germany was well supplied with manufactured and consumer goods. In 1932, out of 1,000 inhabitants, 66 possessed a radio set and 52 a car (the European average was 38 and seven respectively). The great industrialization process had paved the way for mass production and consumption, while urbanization had led to a fall in the self-sufficient home production of goods. The introduction of the 40-hour working week and paid holidays allowed wage-earners to organize their free time. And so the modern idea of leisure time was born, and what had until then been exclusively middle-class luxuries were now virtually within everyone's reach. Amusement parks, variety theatres and dance halls were all the rage. Cinemas, boxing rings and cycling tracks drew increasingly large crowds, especially of young people. Membership of associations of all kinds – working class, youth, women's, cultural and sports – was expanding rapidly. After the crisis of the old liberal and authoritarian models following the mass mobilization of World War I, and as a result of political, socio-cultural and technological transformations, society began took on a new shape. A cry rose up for more ambitious and far-reaching ideas for popular expression than those of the traditional pre-wartime associations; the masses were more willing to participate in large political movements while, at the same time, technology enabling the manipulation of public opinion was now available. These organized masses came to the forefront in large-scale marches and political protests.

AT THE LAKESIDE
Berliners at a café near the city. (Above)

BERLIN VARIETY THEATRE
Dancing girls in their dressing room before going on stage.

Selling Vegetables in a German City

New photographic and cinematographic techniques favoured the development of autonomous styles that were based on the image and, no longer borrowed from literature or theatre, were linked to metropolitan culture. Exponents included directors such as Fritz Lang, Max Ophüls and Friedrich W. Murnau.

A characteristic of much of this culture was its lack of identification with the new republican and democratic values because of the limits of the political reformism of the Social Democrats, limits also evident in their influence on cultural life as well as in their general ideology. Many of the most active and lively intellectuals of this period were highly critical of the new order, which was, in their opinion, unable to represent any truly radical innovation.

The last years of the republic witnessed a turn towards exalting war, preparing the way for and then spreading fascist mentality and ideology. Faced with such polarization and radical views, many intellectuals withdrew from public life at the beginning of the 1930s, preferring to affirm the primacy of the inner self.

Economic Crisis and Unemployment

The economic crisis of 1929 was essentially rooted in the capitalistic and financial development of the United States. The close ties that Germany had with the American economy from the early 1920s meant that it was one of the countries hardest hit by the crisis. The recession in production reached dramatic levels, with consumer goods suffering badly. Wages suffered a sharp decline, partly due to the cut in minimum wage decreed by the government, and partly

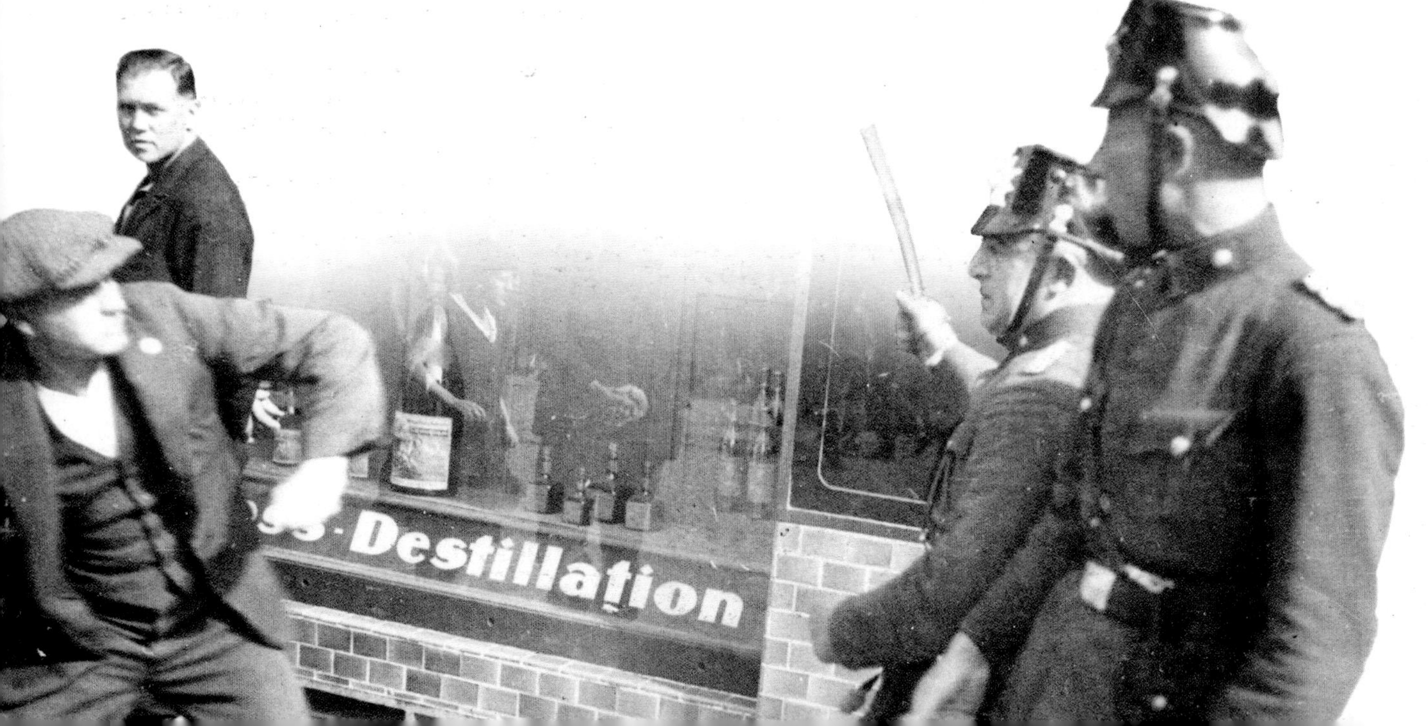

Police against strikers
Triggered by an excess of printed money, the alarming inflation figures of the Weimar years weakened the purchasing power of the mark, hitting especially hard those who depended on a fixed income to survive .
(Below)

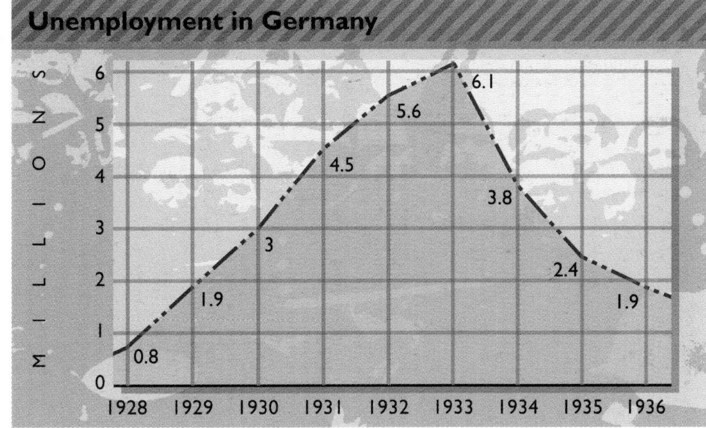

due to the employers' failure to respect collective contracts. At the same time, prices continued to rise. But most alarming of all was the unemployment rate, which grew from 8.5 per cent in 1929 to 29.9 per cent in 1932, equal to roughly five and a half million registered as out of work, plus about a million unregistered.

The hardest hit were blue-collar workers, especially miners and workers in heavy industry, along with white-collar workers. Many public officials did not lose their jobs, but their salaries were cut sharply, while small businesses and shopkeepers were hit by the crash in prices and the decline in the public's buying power. Both unemployment insurance, guaranteed by law since 1927, and emergency benefits lasted for a relatively brief time. To the growing poverty was added a widespread sense of frustration and a lack of optimism that the situation would improve. Along with the economic crisis, the authority of the Weimar Republic was further undermined because of its evident failure to cope with the country's serious social problems. Militarized groups on the right and the left offered the cohesion and opportunity to fill in their empty time that the unemployed did not find elsewhere – the discipline of these organizations substituted the discipline of the workplace. The worldwide economic crisis was one of the fundamental causes of the ultimate collapse of the republic: on the one hand it caused a radicalization of the masses, ready for anything in order to escape from the anguish of the present; on the other, it gave the conservatives the opportunity to strike the final blow against the system created in 1918.

The Growth of the NSDAP

The effects of the Great Depression coincided with the growth in popularity of the Nazi Party, which drew its strength mainly from the progressive weakening of the institutions

Graph Showing Unemployment Figures in Germany 1928–36 (Above)

Horse Carcass by the Roadside
People trying to glean nourishment from the meat of a dead horse.

NAZI PROPAGANDA TRUCK PASSING THROUGH BERLIN'S BRANDENBURG GATE
In the early years, the Nazi Party was often a street-fighting force and an organization whose ideology appealed to conservatives and people who had been hit by the economic crisis.

of the republic and from the downsizing that was taking place in the right wing of the political spectrum. The NSDAP found increasing favour with the population at large, who were becoming disaffected with the idea of democracy; the majority of Germans, tired of unemployment and insecurity, were calling for order of whatever nature, as long as it could guarantee stability for the future. The authoritarian tradition of imperial Germany had very deep roots, and it led the majority of people to believe that the only solution was to return to the principles that the republic had tried to snuff out, without, however, managing to replace them with new ones. The continued growth of the Nazi Party from 1930 on was also helped by the powerlessness shown by the democratic front in dealing with the spread of the economic crisis. The NSDAP reaped great success in the countryside and in small and medium-sized towns, while in the large cities the working-class parties were still fairly strong. The election results from 1930 and 1933 show that the Nazis drew most of their votes from the traditional electorate of the bourgeois forces. The increasing number of its deputies being elected enabled the Nazi Party to use parliament as a platform for its slogans. The growth in party members and supporters was translated into street militancy, which channelled widespread dissatisfaction and rebelliousness. The great skill of the NSDAP lay in its ability to use every possible technique to manipulate collective behaviour. A further essential contribution to its success was made by the key sectors of the German economy which, convinced of the necessity to restore an authoritarian and anti-socialist order, from 1930 on generously financed the Nazi Party.

THE CRUMBLING OF THE REPUBLIC

It was the economic crisis that dealt the death blow to the Weimar Coalition. The debates among the coalition parties

ALFRED HUGENBERG

Born in Hanover in 1865, Alfred Hugenberg was a member of many nationalist circles and organizations from the 1890s onwards. He was a major industrialist who built up an enormous economic empire during the war, thanks mostly to the control he held over large areas of the press and other means of communication which he used with extreme virulence against the newborn Republic. His election to the presidency of the German National Party in 1928 was crucial for concentrating nationalist and pan-Germanic forces around the NSDAP. He financed the Nazi Party in order to exploit its capacity to draw street crowds, planning to use it as a bridgehead to destroy the Weimar system. Hugenberg's economic weight and his political role offered concrete proof that powerful sectors of the economy were behind the growing success of the Nazi Party. It also illustrated that representatives of the conservative parties believed they could exploit the Nazis as an advance force to break the back of the democratic front and then take political power back into their own hands to set up a conservative alignment of the old imperial type which would be more than just a new system of alliances.

Hugenberg's decision to resolve the German crisis with an anti-parliamentary coup gave the nationalist right-wing parties – which all in one way or another aimed at the restoration of an authoritarian regime – the opportunity to overcome their rivalries. The advantage that the NSDAP had over these parties was that it had introduced street violence as a political tool.

In the years to follow, the destiny of Hugenberg's party, which was dissolved shortly after January 1933, highlighted just how illusory the ideals of imperial restoration had been.

CHILDREN WAITING FOR THEIR MILK RATION In the early 1930s, almost one worker in two was unemployed. This was devastating for German families on the lower rungs of society and had the psychological and material effect of worsening the already deep-rooted insecurity that was widely felt throughout the country after the war.

SWASTIKAS ON THE FLAGS
A magic-religious symbol common among peoples of Indo-European languages had its arms extended to become the swastika that the Nazis took as the emblem of their political organization.

NO SPEECH ALLOWED
Hitler is forbidden from speaking in a 1926 Nazi propaganda poster.

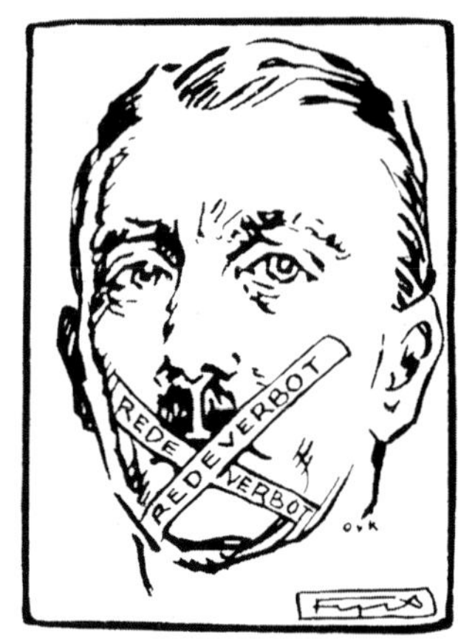

about how to deal with the economic emergency grew increasingly heated and the political struggle took on radical and violent tones. The working-class parties, which still had the majority of the workers' votes, were incapable either of coming to grips with the social and economic emergency or of recognizing the threat represented by the NSDAP. Meanwhile, the Nazis triggered aggressive and violent public demonstrations against the working-class parties and all other movements in any way identified with the democratic system – pacifist organizations, antimilitarist movements and individual intellectuals.

At the level of government, the alignment of forces that was to bury the republic began to take shape. In March of 1930, President Hindenburg gave the Catholic Heinrich Brüning the mandate to form a new government, applying article 48 of the constitution, according to which he would not be responsible to parliament but only to the president. Thus began the period of presidential cabinets which, though perhaps not the inevitable premise of the Nazi triumph, certainly dealt another serious blow to the democratic system of government. Between 1930 and 1933, the conservative forces allied themselves with the Nazi Party, hoping to use it as a battering ram to bring down the existing system and convinced that it would be possible to divest it of its subversive potential and then make it part of a government coalition. The conservatives took the end of the democratic republic as a foregone conclusion. Their failure to fully perceive the subversive and revolutionary nature of the NSDAP meant that after 1933 they, too, were among the victims of its strategy.

MEIN KAMPF

Mein Kampf ('My Battle') was written by Hitler while in prison following the failed Munich Putsch in 1924. The first volume came out in 1925 and the second the following year. It expressed some of the cornerstones of his political and ideological thinking, especially as regards living space and the Jewish question, two issues that were closely linked. 'A state,' he wrote, 'that in an epoch of racial decadence dedicates itself to the care of its best racial elements must one day become master of the world.' The book discussed economic questions only very briefly and in the vaguest of terms. *Mein Kampf* was translated into 16 languages and by 1940, ten million copies had been published. However, it is hard to determine how many people actually read it, and how many among those who read it fully understood its message. Besides, in both demonstrations and propaganda speeches there was always the tendency to tailor words to suit the circumstances of the moment, promising what would obviously please the crowd rather than bothering about whether the promises being made could actually be kept.
However, it would be wrong to think that by 1924 Hitler had clarified all of his future political development. *Mein Kampf* is more a reflection of the main themes of his thinking, much of which became possible to carry out thanks to a series of circumstances that were impossible to foresee in the mid-1920s.

TOWNS AND HOUSING POLICY

Experimentation in town planning that began before the Great War (the garden city movement, company villages and industrial philanthropy, model neighbourhoods) found new vigour in the 1920s in theories that at times were carried out in the form of the 'work city' (*Trabantenstadt*) – the socialist city that represented an alternative to 19th-century bourgeois cities (Ernst May, Ludwig Hilberseimer). The metropolis itself (*Groszstadt*) was no longer taken as a model to be demonized for its great numbers, but rather represented a goal for reform. The city was seen not only as a site for rationalized factories (AEG, Siemens) but also a place for day-to-day living partly freed from work, where even free time could be rationally organized. Examples of this could be found in the model neighbourhoods and schools of Ernst May in Frankfurt, the satellite towns, the parks and bathing establishments of Martin Wagner in Berlin, and the great courts of Fritz Schumacher in Hamburg. These scenarios served as the background for the novels of Alfred Döblin on the dramatic transformations of the urban environment, and for Walter Benjamin's reflections on Berlin in change. Encouraged by a policy of incentives for cooperatives and guaranteed by agreements with the trade unions, housing policy enjoyed a period of experimentation. New neighbourhoods grew up to provide a high quality of life (Berlin Britz by Bruno Taut, for example). The growing need for housing led to mass production (housing factories) and slogans such as *Existenzminimum* were pushed to an extreme. Accordingly, stark sociological parameters were translated into housing requirements to impose minimal living spaces. There were also interesting experiments – carried out with an eye to reform – concerning the rationalization of domestic life and of women's lives; particularly important here was Grete Schütte-Likowsky's *Frankfurter Küche* (Frankfurt Kitchen).

BERLIN'S WERTHEIM EMPORIUM
A place where the capital's middle classes came to shop. (Above)

BELOW: CARL LEGIEN RESIDENTIAL AREA
Berlin's urban architecture was avant-garde in the 1920s.

The 'national revolution'

Between 1932 and 1933 there was still room for a compromise between the political classes, the old social élite and the Nazi Party, which had obtained 18.3 per cent of the vote in the elections for the Reichstag in September 1930. The political alignment that supported the President of the Reich dropped the prejudicial barrier that had so far prevented Hitler from being named Chancellor, convinced that he would be surrounded by trusted men of the right. On 30 January 1933, Marshall Hindenburg gave Hitler the mandate to form the new government. The initial concern of the new Chancellor was to demonstrate a moderate approach. His cabinet was formed by a minority of Nazis, along with representatives of the various elements of the conservative right as well as the armed forces, who were still confident they could keep the situation under control. Franz von Papen as Vice-Chancellor, Hugenberg as Minister for the Economy, Werner von Blomberg as Defence Minister and Franz Seldte as Minister of Labour

Chancellor Hitler and President Hindenburg in 1933 (Page 32)

The Parliament Burning (Page 33)

Propaganda
A Nazi poster accusing the Communists of having set the Reichstag on fire, and canvassing votes for the party headed by Hitler.

National Revolution
A Nazi poster gets its point across with a simple slogan.

seemed a large enough group to dilute any extreme overtures made by Frick, the National Socialist Home Minister, and Hermann Göring, Minister Without Portfolio. But in just a few months the so-called 'national revolution' was set into motion, going well beyond the conservatives' plans and transforming the concession of power into the seizure of power. The alliance of the economic élite, the army and the NSDAP – whose common goals were the destruction of the working-class movement, the establishment of a dictatorship and the forced acceleration of rearmament – would eventually provide the power structure of the Third Reich. At the beginning of 1933, the leaders of the workers' parties and the trade unions were resigned and passive, and the anti-fascist parties had been unable to grasp the speed and nature of the changes taking place. Entrenched in contrasting positions, they were unable to agree on a common strategy. On 30 January 1933, the initiative for action had firmly passed to the Nazi Party.

The Burning of the Reichstag

On the night of 27 February 1933, the Reichstag was burnt down. The finger of blame was pointed to the Dutch Communist Martin Van der Lubbe, who was arrested and sentenced to death. The question of who was really responsible for the incident remains uncertain. What is clear, however, is that the new government ably exploited the situation. Next day, Hitler persuaded Hindenburg to sign a 'decree for the protection of the people and the state', initiating a set of austere measures that abolished certain fundamental principles. Freedom of thought, of the press and of association, and the secrecy of written correspondence and the inviolability of the home were all suspended. In addition, penalties for certain charges were stiffened, to the point that in some cases the death penalty was reintroduced. Arrest for reasons of security was legalized as a preventative measure, allowing political enemies to be held; this measure was adopted

A Pile of Rubble
This was all that remained of the Reichstag after the fire on 27 February 1933. This criminal act was exploited by Hitler to pass a decree severely restricting civil and political liberties and reinstating the death penalty.

FRANZ VON PAPEN
Leader of the country for a few months in 1932, von Papen presided over the death throes of the Weimar Republic and gave *carte blanche* to the Nazi paramilitary squads. He was appointed vice-chancellor in Hitler's first cabinet.

ELECTORAL POSTERS

HITLER MAKING HIS ENTRANCE AT A NAZI RALLY IN 1933
(Below)

in particular against Communists. The decree signed on 28 February in no way subordinated the Chancellor to the authority of the President of the Reich; thus, the state of emergency that characterized the entire duration of the Nazi regime was institutionalized.

The elections held on 5 March took place in a climate of terrorist violence. But the 43.99 per cent of the vote procured by the NSDAP was not enough for it to secure the absolute majority it was hoping for. On 23 March, the parliament, by now purged of the Communist Party, met again to vote on a law giving full powers to the Führer, thereby laying the foundations for strengthening the executive and definitively dismantling the Weimar system. The law was approved with 444 votes in favour and 94 against. The only ones to vote against it were the Social Democrats and their president, Otto Wels, who courageously denounced the death of democracy. The representatives of all the other parties approved the new law, convinced that a strong executive was needed to guarantee a return to order. From here on, the parliament met only on rare occasions and exclusively to applaud and ratify decisions taken by the Führer.

PURGING STATE AND SOCIETY

The hope that was held by the conservative forces that they could dominate the Nazi Party and mould it to their own interests was soon dashed. On 9 March, the parliamentary mandate of the Communists was annulled, and many

'HITLER: OUR LAST CHANCE'

SOCIAL DEMOCRAT EQUALS JEW
The wording 'I, great nephew of Mordechai-Marx have given you my symbol' makes a sarcastic allusion to the Jewish side-locks which, turning into arrows, became the symbol of the German Social Democrats.

SA PARADE
The placards say, 'Don't buy from Jews!' (Below)

representatives and party officials were arrested or forced into exile. The Social Democrats, determined to remain within the limits of the law, had nonetheless sent some of its most important members out of the country. When the party was outlawed on 22 June, the leadership decided to continue its anti-Nazi struggle from abroad. The remaining parties disbanded, and by the end of June the Nazis represented the only legal political force in Germany. For those who had worked against the regime, the situation became more and more dangerous; many intellectuals went into exile to escape the growing threat and to be able to continue to give free voice to their denunciation of what was happening in their native country.

On 7 April, a law was passed 'for the revival of the professional bureaucracy', which aimed at subordinating the administrative machinery to the orders of the new regime. All officials who had taken up service after 9 November 1918 were dismissed, along with anyone who was of 'non-Aryan' origin. So, even before any racist legislation was drawn up, its underlying principle was rooted in a vital sector of the state. At the same time, street violence, which up until then had been aimed mainly at the working-class parties, began to be directed against Jews. On 1 April, a boycott of Jewish shops was staged, inaugurating a series of actions that was coordinated by the government. Although this initiative was not particularly successful, growing sections of the population were starting to be convinced of the guilt and inferiority of the Jews.

NAZISM AND THE CHURCH

In the first years of Hitler's government, the Catholic and Protestant churches played an important role in reinforcing the authority of the Nazi state and in stamping out every possible flashpoint of opposition. Within just a few months,

THE BONFIRE OF BOOKS

On 10 May 1933, thousands of books by authors such as Sigmund Freud, Karl Marx, Erich Maria Remarque, Carl von Ossietzky and Kurt Tucholsky were set on fire in the public squares of many university towns. The fires had been organized by the students' leagues, and the majority of professors took part, making it clear that there would be no opposition to the new regime from the universities. But despite what it was made to seem, this was no spontaneous gesture revealing the true feelings of German students. On the contrary, it was an event deliberately planned and coordinated by Joseph Goebbels who, from a podium in Berlin, delivered a violently abusive attack on the condemned authors. The fires represented not only a barbarian act, but also the ambition of the Nazi government to seize cultural hegemony. Images of flames turning books to ashes were published all over Europe, and aroused profound indignation. Many German intellectuals in exile saw in this act a further confirmation that they had made the right choice to leave. On the first anniversary of this episode a year later, a group of intellectuals led by Heinrich Mann inaugurated the German Liberty Library (Deutsche Freiheitsbibliothek) in Paris. This library was intended to show that the real German spirit had not been burnt, but only silenced in its native country.

MACABRE PROCESSION
University professors and students parade around a bonfire of books. This was a clear sign of the terror that the Nazis were about to unleash. (Above)

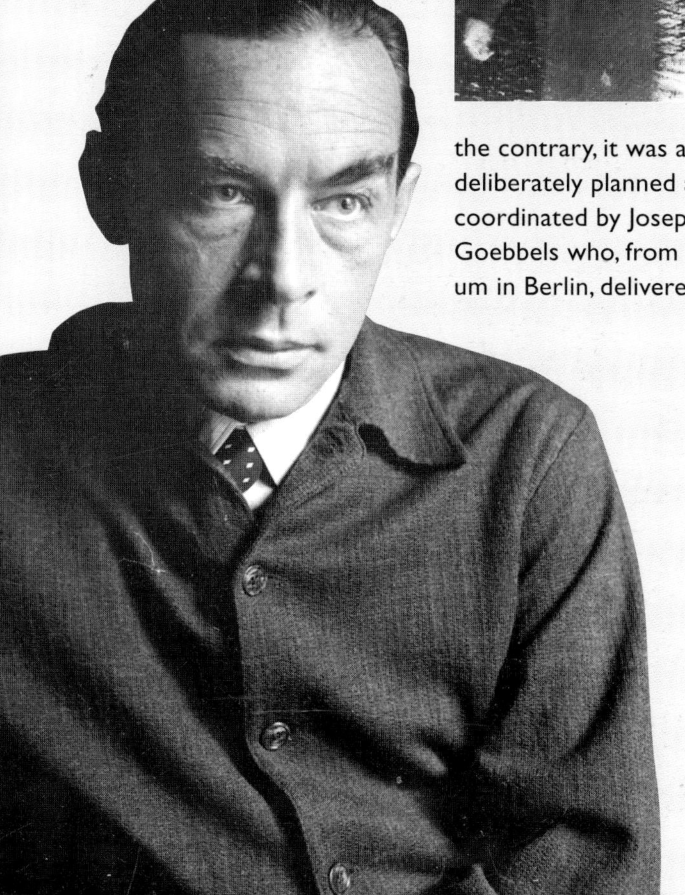

ERICH MARIA REMARQUE
One of the writers whose books were burned in German squares in May 1933.

ADOLF HITLER

Adolf Hitler was born in 1889 in the Austrian town of Brunau am Inn. Son of a customs official and his third wife, Hitler applied for admission to the Academy of Fine Arts in Vienna following his father's death, but was rejected. He earned a living as a house painter and postcard illustrator. In 1913, he moved to Munich and at the outbreak of war the following year, he enrolled as a volunteer. At the end of the war he returned to Munich, where he joined a reserve battalion and began to take interest in extreme right-wing politics. In 1919, he joined the German Workers' Party, which changed its name to the NSDAP (National Socialist German Workers' Party). His prestige within the party continued to grow, and after his imprisonment for his part in the Munich Putsch, he became its uncontested leader. After the 1930 elections, the NSDAP assumed the features of a major party, with 107 representatives in parliament, and Hitler entered the right-wing front (the Harzburg Front). In 1932 he obtained German nationality and so gained the right to aspire to become Chancellor, a post that was entrusted to him by President Hindenburg the following year.

The stages that marked his climb to political success coincided with the dismantling of the democratic system and the concentration of all state power in his hands, a process that concluded in 1934. Over the next few years, his power and prestige continued to grow, partly because he managed to remain distanced from any conflicts that arose, whether those within the Nazi élite or those of a more general political nature. The myth created around his image was one of the most formidable propaganda instruments of the Third Reich, and it was only questioned during World War II, when it was no longer possible to make people believe that the situation could change for the better.

When Hitler moved from Vienna to Munich in 1913, his ideological baggage was confused, founded on anti-Semitism and racist imperialism. The fact that he was able to become the leader of the most powerful party in Germany and to guide its destiny for 12 years can be attributed to three factors: the unrelenting opposition to the Weimar Republic by a sizeable section of the conservative elements of society; the growing dissatisfaction felt by large sectors of the population, caused mainly by the deepening economic crisis; and Hitler's genius as an orator, which turned him into a quasi-Messiah in the eyes of the many Germans who wanted improvement in their own lives. There is nothing inexplicable, therefore, in his incredible rise to power: it was simply the result of a complex and multi-faceted combination of circumstances.

Acting Rehearsal
'Apocalyptic, visionary, convincing'; these are the captions (from left to right) of the photographs taken by Heinrich Hoffman in 1925. (Above)

Hitler at Nuremberg

CHILDREN WAVING SWASTIKA FLAGS AS THE FÜHRER PASSES BY

ITALIAN ARCHBISHOP
Eugenio Pacelli – the future Pope Pius XII – was Papal Nuncio during the 1920s, first in Munich then in Berlin. (Below)

relations with both denominations – one third of Christians were Catholic, the other two-thirds were Protestant – were made clear. A law passed on 14 July 1933 put an end to the organization of Protestantism into 28 churches, replacing it with a unitary structure guided by a bishop of the Reich according to a model that clearly evoked the *Führerprinzip*. This had been done thanks to an initiative promoted by a Protestant group, the *Deutsche Christen*, who favoured an authoritarian state and supported Nazi policy in the following years, to the point of advocating discrimination against the Jews. The Protestants who opposed this view formed the 'Confessional Church', whose synod of May 1934 espoused the position that even a totalitarian state had to recognize the divine commandments as a limit. In the years to follow, the Confessional Church was mainly concerned with defending its own field of action, although it did at times go further towards a more radical form of opposition.

In the first months of 1933, the Catholic Church came under heavy attack from the regime: measures introduced that would seriously limit its behaviour included propaganda against Catholic schools, attacks against its press, and growing limits placed on the freedom of its associations. On 20 July, an agreement between Hitler's government and the Holy See was signed that was meant to regulate their relations in the following years.

According to this agreement, which undoubtedly contributed to the growing international prestige of Nazism, the state recognized the Church's freedom of religion and its right to have its own schools and associations, as long as they were limited to cultural and charitable ends. On its part, the Holy See prohibited the clergy from taking part in any type of political activity. But in the years to follow, the Nazi regime did not stick to these stipulations, and opposition among Catholics grew accordingly.

An SA Unit Advertising a Lottery

Gregor Strasser
A top Nazi leader (pictured left), Strasser called for a social shift towards the 'national revolution'. He was assassinated in the 'night of the long knives'. (Below left)

Hitler and Ernst Röhm
Röhm became head of the SA in 1931; two years later the organization counted some two million members. (Below right)

The Night of the Long Knives

There were many different political ideals within the Nazi Party. In July of 1933, after the disappearance of the last potential challenger to the Nazi Party, the Catholic Centre Party, Hitler declared that the phase of the 'revolution' was over, and it was now time for 'evolution'. This point of view was not shared by Ernst Röhm, head of the SA and leader of the rank-and-file party movement, who was determined to use the paramilitary organization that he headed to keep the party's activist and revolutionary spirit alive. He considered the SA the nucleus of a future popular militia which would be in opposition to the army. That the party should fit into the traditional apparatus of power in no way corresponded to his ideals, and even less so did the proclaimed end of its revolutionary phase.

Meanwhile, thanks to President Hindenburg's mediation, the ties between Hitler and the *Reichswehr* were tightened, while personalities such as Joseph Goebbels, Hermann Göring and Heinrich Himmler – each of them interested in increasing his own sphere of influence – wanted to neutralize the SA and Röhm's projects for a 'second revolution'. Hitler himself was convinced of the need to do away with Röhm, whom he considered a potential subversive who represented a threat to his increasingly tight alliance with the conservative groups.

With the false justification that the SA was organizing a coup d'état, Röhm was murdered along with over 100 other members of the SA on the night of 30 June 1934 in an event known as the 'night of the long knives'. In this way many potentially dangerous adversaries were eliminated, and the most radical element of the party, which had been strongest in the Weimar years, was wiped out. Hindenburg thanked Hitler for having saved the country, and the general staff of the army did not intervene – even though two generals had

PAUL VON HINDENBURG

Born in 1847, von Hindenburg was the son of an officer and was introduced to a military career at an early age. He fought in the Franco-Prussian War of 1870, which marked the start of his climb up to the highest ranks of the German army. He retired in 1908 but was called back into service at the outbreak of World War I. From 1916 on, he was commander-in-chief of the army; together with General Erich Ludendorff he played a major role in the war, putting into practice some of the earliest techniques of total warfare. After the war, he contributed to spreading the myth of an army that had not been beaten in the field, thereby fostering mistrust of the newborn Weimar Republic. When he was elected President in 1925, he disappointed many conservatives because he remained faithful to the parliamentary government and gave his support to Stresemann's foreign policy. After the appointment of Brüning as Chancellor in 1930, Hindenburg was far more directly involved in the conduct of political life, trying to push it to the right without abandoning the foundations of the constitution. He was re-elected in 1932 with the votes of the Social Democrats and the Catholic centre, who had not supported him in previous elections. Behind the figure of Hindenburg was the political and economic influence of the major landholders from east Germany, who were openly hostile to democracy. Hindenburg represented a fundamental link between the conservative agricultural world and the growing Nazi movement, which, from the end of the 1920s, witnessed a boom of consensus in the countryside. After the nomination of Hitler as Chancellor, Hindenburg retired from politics. He died a year later.

With Hitler and Göring
Hindenburg decreed that the posts of Chancellor and President of the Reich should be united in the figure of Hitler. (Above)

With a Boy from the Hitler Youth Movement

Germany is Free!
The image of the Führer dominates a poster in 1934.

The Reichswehr and the SA
A parade of army units is followed by the SA. The link between the armed forces and paramilitary groups ensured that the growing Nazi Party had significant strength. (Below)

been murdered – and the churches were silent. Violence and illegality had now been established as instruments of government.

The Totalitarian State

The law proclaimed on 14 July 1933 sanctioned the existence of one party and one alone. Local, regional and municipal autonomies were revoked. This was another step towards the removal of all forms of independence and diversity and a reinforcement of the central government's power of control. As a confirmation of the ever-growing merging of state and party, the post of *Gauleiter* was created, at once party leader and head of an administrative area. The legislative autonomy of the *Länder* (regions) was gradually weakened until it was completely abolished under the terms of a January 1934 law that created the structure of the Reich. The concentration of all authority in the hands of Adolf Hitler reached its conclusion during the course of that year. The elimination of Röhm and his followers was a fundamental milestone in this process.

After the death of President Hindenburg, Hitler took on the title of President of the Reich and Commander in Chief of the Armed Forces along with that of Chancellor. The construction of the role of Führer was now complete, not only inside the party but also within the state institutions. The principle of the leader (*Führerprinzip*) became the foundation of Nazi power: the pyramidal power structure peaked at the Führer, charismatic and supreme leader, the source of law and the basis of the legitimacy of the dictatorship. The model that governed the summit of the Reich was reproduced at every political and administrative level, with the obligation of obedience all the way up the hierarchy. Besides being the unquestioned leader of the party, Hitler gave himself the power to control the entire state apparatus. A year and a half after

Nazi Medals and Badges

SA Saluting Hitler
Convinced that destiny had chosen him to lead the country, Adolf Hitler skilfully exploited the desire of the German people to have a charismatic figurehead. (Below)

Hitler became head of the government, the Nazi regime concluded the construction of its new institutional order.

Nazi Ideology

One of the core beliefs of Nazi ideology was the racial question. In Hitler's opinion – as he had written in *Mein Kampf* – there were superior and inferior races, and it was essential to avoid contact between them to prevent the bastardization of the superior races. The German people were, in his opinion, made up of an as yet 'uncontaminated' majority and it was necessary to guarantee that only this majority could reproduce so that the Germanic people could become purer and purer. This gradual 'purification' was, however, threatened by the Jews, who were responsible not only for the outbreak of World War I, but also for the defeat of the Reich and the proclamation of the republic. Fighting the Jews, therefore, meant saving the Aryan identity of the German people, who were engaged in a struggle to defend themselves against an underhand conspiracy against the nation.

The other core element of Nazi ideology was the conviction that Germany had to expand outside the borders of its own territory by taking over areas in the East so as to guarantee a greater abundance of raw materials and vital resources. Therefore, the Treaty of Versailles had to be annulled, and it was

Rudolf Hess
Arrested after the failed Munich Putsch, Hess helped Hitler draft *Mein Kampf*. He later became Hitler's personal secretary and accumulated vast powers within the Nazi Party.

NSDAP Flag

Anniversary of the Munich Putsch
Top Nazi Party leaders parade through the streets of the city. (Below)

time for Germany to take on the mantle of a great power once again. The USSR, which Hitler viewed as being ruled by a cabal of shady Jewish businessmen, was the quintessential evil, and Hitler's continual barbs against it confirm how racism was the essence of his expansionist policy. His position regarding other aspects of life in the German state were also based on racism. The youth, for example, had to maintain racial purity and their bodies were to be trained – mainly through sport – for the use of force and aggression. The role of women was reduced to the purely biological function of procreating sons for the fatherland.

The strong point of this type of ideology lay above all in its capacity to catalyse public opinion, to substitute a system of values in crisis and present itself as a supreme truth. This was a new anti-democratic ideology that replaced discredited values with a unification of theory and practice destined to reinforce its credibility.

Symbols and Rites in the Nazy Party

The merging of state and party was also evident on a symbolic level. On 12 March 1933, President Hindenburg decreed that alongside the black, white and red flag of the Reich should be flown a flag adorned with the swastika. On 21 May, the new Reichstag met for the first time in the Potsdam church that held the tomb of Frederick II. The so-called 'Potsdam Day', with its symbolic appeal to Prussian traditions, was aimed at stirring up nationalistic fervour in the service of the new regime.

A key occasion for the party to display its symbols was its congresses, which were not conceived of as occasions for political debate, but rather as self-exaltation, an expression of power and a concrete demonstration of the existence of the 'popular community'. Thus the congresses took on the character of state celebrations and each one took the title of mottos that recalled important times of the past: in 1933, it

SA UNITS PARADE AT NUREMBERG An army in everything but name, the NSDAP initially won control of the streets. Its permanent state of rebellion, however, made it enemies both within the SS and the *Reichswehr*, who found it hard to live with the armed organization after Hitler came to power.

1 May 1936: Hitler's Speech at the Lustgarten in Berlin
After trade unions were banned on 2 May 1933 and their assets confiscated, National Work Day was inaugurated and the German labour front was established, encompassing blue- and white-collar workers as well as entrepreneurs. (Below)

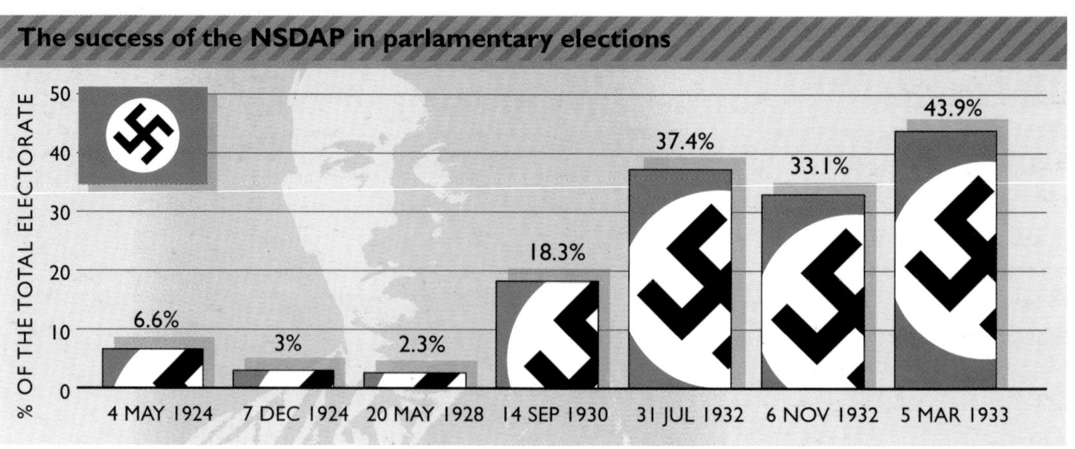

was 'Victory of the Faith' to celebrate the Nazi's rise to power, and the 1934 congress was called 'Triumph of the Will' to indicate the completion of the process of takeover of the state apparatus. In 1935, the architect Albert Speer created an enormous space in Nuremburg with a stadium, a congress hall and enormous fields where columns of faithful servants of the state marched. Every year in September, surrounded by a sea of flags, the SS, the SA, the youth organizations and units of the Wehrmacht paraded in front of the Führer. Sports events, speeches and marches all culminated with a speech delivered by Hitler.

To heighten the theatrical effects of this production even further, Goebbels, able stage director that he was, made sure the congresses were announced and prepared with a relentless press campaign that ensured a vast audience. The regime also introduced a new holiday for its own celebration during which the ideological revolution was reasserted. The first of May became 'National Work Day', though the workers were no longer mentioned and the traditional anniversary of international workers' solidarity was ignored. On the second sunday of May, Mothers' Day was celebrated, with speeches and demonstrations that reiterated the central role of women as mothers of numerous offspring for the German nation. Hitler's birthday (20 April) offered another occasion for the regime to reinforce the myth of the Führer, and was celebrated all over Germany with military parades and dancing.

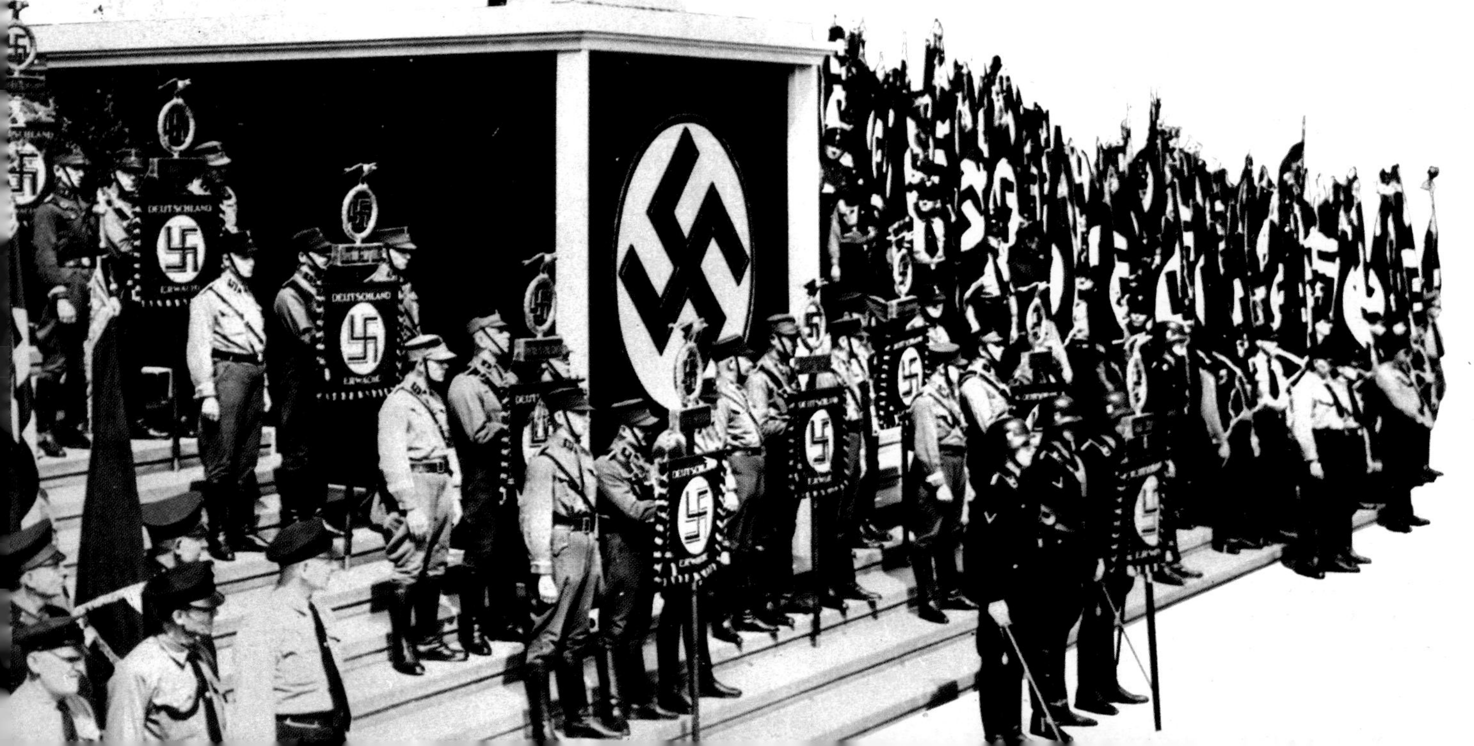

JOSEPH GOEBBELS

Born into a Catholic family in 1897, Goebbels saw his request to volunteer for the war rejected on the grounds that he was lame. He studied German philosophy and art history, and after his degree tried unsuccessfully to become a journalist and a playwright. In 1924, he joined the NSDAP and at once became one of its most prolific journalists, working for numerous Nazi periodicals. At first he supported the party's left wing, whose leader was Gregor Strasser, but in 1926 he became a follower of Hitler as well as *Gauleiter* of Berlin, where his talents as a demagogic orator soon came to the fore. His capacity for organization and propaganda became evident when he exploited the death of the young SA, Horst Wessel, making him into a martyr of the movement. This was the first of a series of myths created by Goebbels in the course of his career. In 1928, he was elected member of parliament for the NSDAP. The following year he was appointed as head of propaganda for the Party, and from then on his activism knew no rest. His best-known initiative at this time was organizing the boycott of the pacifist film *All Quiet on the Western Front*, which was based on the novel by Erich Maria Remarque. After the Nazis took power, he was named Minister of Propaganda and head of the Chamber of Culture, becoming the undisputed leader of cultural life under the regime. Quite unsurpassed as a skilled manipulator of the masses, he invented new forms of self-representation for the regime, dedicating himself to anti-Semitic propaganda that was characterized by its extremely aggressive and vulgar language. He was the organizer of the 'night of the broken glass' and of the exhibition of 'degenerate art'. During World War II, writing mainly from the columns of the weekly *Das Reich*, he raised the level of the regime's propaganda to fever pitch, focusing his attentions on the Bolshevik enemy. After the defeat at Stalingrad, he instigated the term 'total war', and in September 1943 tried in vain to convince Hitler to sign a separate peace. In the last days of the regime he was one of Hitler's most faithful followers, remaining with him in the bunker until the end. His diaries, written regularly from 1923 with the aim of creating a posthumous image of himself as a great political guide, represent one of the most insightful sources of information on the power apparatus of the Nazi regime.

Minister of Propaganda and Skilled Orator

The author Thomas Mann wrote in 1933: 'Enough of this boorish head of hellish propaganda, this cripple in body and soul who aims with inhuman baseness to raise untruth to divine heights and world sovereignty!'

Goebbels' Motto

'Only serenity and a heart of iron will lead us to victory.'

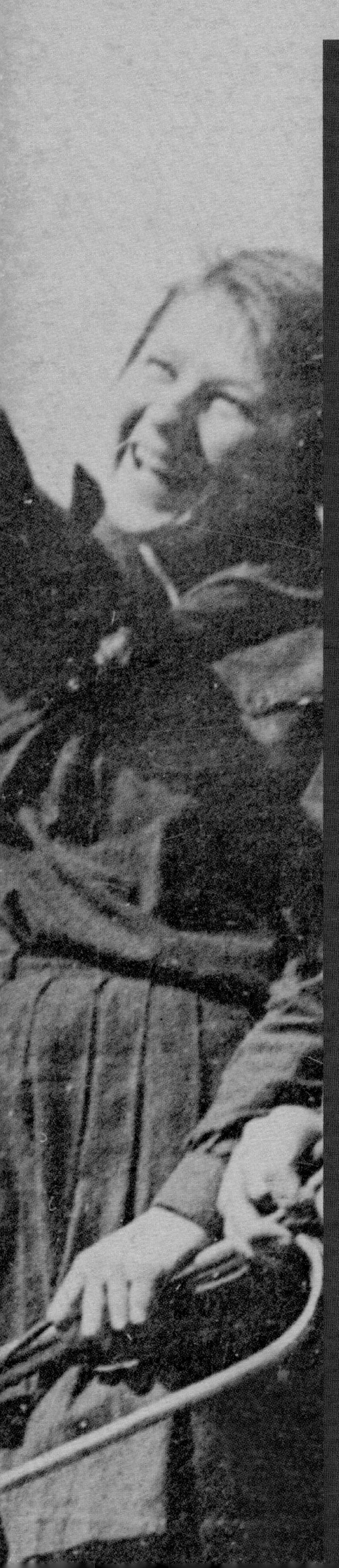

The organization of society

An extensive use of propaganda was one of the features that characterized the Nazi Party, both during its early years as a political movement and later when in power. It knew how to make use of the most advanced techniques for moulding consensus. In the 1920s, the German state had resorted to propaganda on a large scale, not to promote individual parties but to bolster the system itself, to make it seem as though it was protecting the interests of the various classes – the supreme authority for safeguarding social integration and the guarantor of political pluralism. After 1933, Hitler's regime broke with this tradition and placed monopoly of information and the control of public opinion as central pillars of its system of

ADULATION OF THE FÜHRER
(Page 48)

YOUNG COMMUNIST PIONEERS IN THE TWENTIES
(Opening page)

MILITARY PARADE
Rearmament and the resulting growth of the whole armaments industry helped to consolidate the support of the military top brass around Hitler.

power. The uniformity of all propaganda and cultural information created a single concept of the world subordinated to the requirements of the regime.

The architect of all this was Joseph Goebbels. He had shown his skill as an organizer of NSDAP activities and he took personal charge of the entire ideological machine of the Reich. One of the fundamental steps in this direction was a law passed in November 1933 that established a Reich Chamber of Culture to control seven chambers covering cinema, theatre, music, press, radio, literature and art. Anyone who wished to work in these professions had to be admitted to the relative chamber. Goebbels thus assured himself overall power of popular culture, and this process of homogenization grew hand in hand with the expulsion from the political and cultural arena of anyone who was out of step with the model of uniformity set by the regime.

YOUTH

Educating the nation's youth was an area to which Nazism attached great importance: the young people of Germany were an enormous, strategic mass to be manipulated, the freshness of their ideals and their enthusiasm there to be taken advantage of. But they were first and foremost the army of the future, who had to be educated for the battle to conquer *Lebensraum* for the German Reich. The regime used the centralized youth organization rather than schools as a lever for exercising control. Males and females were kept strictly separate: boys were enrolled in the *Hitlerjugend*, while girls joined the *Bund Deutscher Mädel (BDM)*. From 1936 onwards, no other youth organization was tolerated and from this point on the Nazi Party had direct control over the way young Germans were allowed to develop.

Obedience, comradeship and a sense of duty were the

THOUSANDS OF YOUNG PEOPLE GIVING THE NAZI SALUTE
Hitler in a *Hitlerjugend* rally drive-past. The collective disciplining of youth was one of the cornerstones of the Nazi regime's activities. Youth were indoctrinated with propaganda and were trained in a Spartan way of living that prepared them for subsequent enrolment in the armed forces.

BALDUR VON SCHIRACH

Baldur von Schirach was born in Berlin in 1905. His father was a captain in the cavalry who became embittered with the newborn republic after being demoted. From early childhood, Baldur attended schools and frequented circles that were profoundly anti-Semitic. He joined the NSDAP in 1925 and three years later rose to head the league of Nazi students. In 1929, he established a newspaper that would later become one of the most widely read in the country – the *Akademischer Beobachter* – and he published books of propaganda for the Nazi youth such as *Der Triumph des Willens. Kampf und Aufstieg Adolf Hitlers und Seiner Regierung* (1933; *The Triumph of Will. The Battle and Rise of Hitler and his Government*) and *Hitler, wie ihn Keiner Kennt Hitler* (1935; *The Hitler Nobody Knows*). In 1931, he was appointed head of the Nazi youth movement, a post he held all through the 1930s. He managed to broaden his authority and political weight while all the other youth organizations were disbanded until, in 1936, the *Hitlerjugend* became the country's only youth organization and Schirach one of the most powerful officials of the state. When war broke out, he volunteered for the armed forces and fought on the Western Front. In 1940, he was appointed head of the annexed area of Vienna and from 1941, he was placed in charge of deporting Jews from the area. However, he became increasingly critical of Hitler and his anti-Semitic policies and the Nazi attitude towards people living in regions to the east of Germany. As a result, he was removed from his post in 1943 and went to live in Tyrol until the end of the war. Sentenced to 20 years imprisonment at the Nuremberg trials for crimes against humanity, he was released in 1966 and died in 1974. He will forever be associated with the tireless work he carried out with the youth organization, and for his skill at indoctrinating a whole generation with the cult of the Führer.

BALDUR VON SCHIRACH
The head of the Hitler Youth (left) movement made extensive use of rituals and mass choreography – which had been part of German youth groups since the 1920s – to reinforce the regime's ideology.

TRUMPETERS
Boys in the Hitler Youth were divided into two age groups: ten to 14 and 15 to 18.

Youth Festival
German boys and girls depicted around a bonfire in a poster from 1934. Five years later, the number of girls belonging to the *Bund Deutscher Mädel* – about $1\frac{1}{2}$ million – was almost equal to the number of boys in the Hitler Youth.

Games and Drills
Rituals and training for young people involved a mix of romanticism with a dash of paganism, militarism and exaggerated patriotism. (Below)

supreme values taught. All the members were classed by age and dressed in uniforms that had to emphasize their belonging to the community of people. At least twice a week, the boys had to take part in marches, sports events and various types of ritual such as role-call at flag-raising ceremonies. The militarization of the youth was promoted by the *Hitlerjugend*, which had a rigid disciplinary system and an internal judicial system that was separate from traditional justice. Propaganda constantly emphasized the organization's youthfulness, but the slogan of 'youth guided by youth' was wholly misleading because the leaders were appointed by the Nazi Party and the structure was rigidly hierarchical. The *Hitlerjugend* eventually comprised eight million boys.

Emblem of the League of Nazi Women

'All Ten-year-old Girls Join the BDM!'
Poster of a joyous member of the Bund Deutscher Mädel, portrayed according to the dictates of youthful Nazi beauty.

The indoctrination of the BDM was much more controversial and contradictory because the typically male jingoistic indoctrination of the *Hitlerjugend* was in open contradiction to the ideals of wife and mother that the regime was attempting to promote. The number of girls enrolled in the Nazi organizations remained a minority and they became an élite cadre.

Women

The function of women in the German Reich can only be understood within the eugenic racist objectives of the regime. Women were viewed exclusively as mothers and educators of their children, but at the same time underdog wives who submitted to male predominance. Procreation for the fatherland was the highest ideal a woman could and should aspire to – provided, naturally, that they represented the highest Aryan racial purity. Idealizing maternity was the excuse for introducing Mother's Day, and from 1938 the Cross of Merit was awarded to the most prolific bearers of children; almost five million were awarded up to September 1941.

Here, too, propaganda was imbued with war-mongering, as can be seen from Hitler's words at the 1938 Nuremberg congress: 'I would be ashamed to be a German man if, in the event of war breaking out, a single German woman were to go to the front. Women have their battlefield too. They play their part for the nation with every son they bring into the world for the nation. Men play their part for the nation just as women do for the family. Equality of rights for women means receiving the appreciation they are due in the vital areas nature has appointed them to.' This meant women losing their autonomy. It was as though all the battles for female emancipation – which had brought significant social and

League of German Women
The regime prohibited women to use cosmetics and show off their feminine beauty, both considered examples of 'Jewish cosmopolitanism'. A new 'German style' required women to dress in a way that ruled out garments considered decadent or that imitated male fashion. (Left)

Awarding Iron Crosses to German Mothers

GERTRUD SCHOLTZ -KLINK

Born in Baden in 1902, Scholtz-Klink joined the NSDAP in 1928. In 1929, following in the footsteps of her first husband who was a local party leader, she set up an organization of national socialist women, firstly in Offenburg and then in other cities in south-west Germany. In October 1930, she became head of the Order of German Women in Baden, a group that had been affiliated to the NSDAP since 1928. Following the unification of all Nazi women's organizations, in 1931 Scholtz-Klink became director of the Association of National Socialist Women of Bavaria and Hesse. In 1934, she became the association's director-general and also leader of the female department of the labour front. During the 1930s, her responsibilities within the party structure were far-reaching, but she was always subjected to male élites, confirming the subordination of women to men in the Third Reich. It was precisely because Scholtz-Klink accepted this state of affairs that her career was brilliant compared to many of her colleagues who were less willing to accept a position of inferiority. She, on the other hand, acknowledged that women needed to be inferior to men in family and personal relationships, and also to the Führer, and she constantly emphasized this belief. After the war, she lived for three years under a false name. She was sentenced to 18 months imprisonment by a French tribunal. After the fall of the Third Reich, she remained one of Nazism's most fanatical and ingenuous supporters, as evidenced in the book she published in 1978, *Die Frau in Dritten Reich (The Women of the Third Reich)*.

Poster for Recruiting German Girls into the Hitler Youth Movement

Gertrud Scholtz-Klink
Scholtz-Klink headed a mass organization that presided over every area of German women's lives.

All of Germany Listens to the Führer on the Radio
Official iconography never tired of portraying the family listening to the voice of the regime's leader. This showed the extent to which this means of mass communication – there were over 8 million radio sets in 1938 – was essential for maintaining harmony between the leader and his people.

Telefunken T121
Posing beside a radio set. (Below)

political conquests during the Weimar years – had never happened. Women were deprived of the right to vote and were discouraged from working by a series of measures ranging from forcing them to turn their job over to their husband, to being forced to take massive wage cuts, to actually being prohibited from taking up certain professions. This situation, however, underwent radical change during World War II when it became necessary to replace the men fighting at the front; then, and in particular when all-out war was declared in 1943, wives and mothers were called back to make their contribution to the fatherland by working.

Radio and Press

Radio was the Nazi Party's most important means of mass communication and it became a tool used daily for propaganda and entertainment. This was made easier through the widespread availability of relatively cheap radio sets. Indeed, the number of people possessing one rose from 25 per cent of the population in 1933 to 70 per cent in 1939. It became mandatory to listen to it, and radio listening groups were fostered, especially during the broadcasts of demonstrations or during factory work-breaks.

Attempting to control the press was more complicated. There were 3,400 newspapers in 1933 and the Nazis were in charge of only a very few of them. However, in just a few months, left-wing papers were outlawed, resulting in many Jews and 'undesirables' losing their jobs.

In 1935, Max Amann, President of the Press Chamber, launched a systematic campaign to bring newspapers into the hands of the state, which resulted in the NSDAP controlling more than 13 million of the almost 20 million newspapers printed daily. In the summer of 1939, there were still

A FRAME FROM *TRIUMPH DES WILLENS* (TRIUMPH OF WILL)
100,000 members of the SA and the SS line up in Nuremberg stadium in 1934.

LENI RIEFENSTHAL
The director walks between Goebbels and Hitler. (Below)

2,200 newspapers in private hands, which not only fostered the impression of moderation, especially abroad, but also because their most important shareholders included industrial groups such as the chemical giant IG Farben.

Nazi control over newspapers increased during the war and many local papers were shut down. In a very short space of time, Goebbels managed to impose absolute uniformity of news. Press conferences were reduced to daily communiqués specifying what was to be printed and what was not, with painstaking detail given to wording. A measure dated October 1933 freed journalists from responsibility to their editors and made them direct employees of the Ministry of Propaganda.

LITERATURE AND THEATRE

The book-burning that took place on 10 May 1933 was a tragic symbol of a regime aiming to suppress freedom of expression. Blacklists of forbidden authors were drawn up and their books banned from libraries, publishing houses, distribution companies and bookshops; by the end of 1934, more than 4,000 books had been banned. Literature was encouraged to exalt the new values – racial purity, the cult of war and the struggle against the Judea-Bolshevis – and both state and party structures organized initiatives, from increasing the number of literary prizes to explicitly steering authors to write about certain topics.

When the economic crisis abated towards the mid-1930s, book production rose, and the publishing industry experienced something of a boom period. The price it paid, however, was a significant decline in editorial independence. The number of books openly praising the regime did, though, remain modest. The major writers, from Thomas Mann to Anna Seghers, Bertolt Brecht to Stephan Zweig, had

LENI RIEFENSTAHL

Leni Riefenstahl was born into a middle-class family in 1902. She studied at the Berlin Academy of Fine Art, specializing in dance. She worked as a dancer and actress in the 1920s, and in 1932 made her debut as a film director with *Das Blaue Licht (The Blue Light)*, which enjoyed a modicum of success through Riefenstahl's imaginative use of the camera. Hitler was impressed by her talent and

asked her to collaborate with him. In 1934, she filmed *Triumph des Willens (Triumph of Will)*, a documentary about the Congress of Nuremberg, which went on to become one of the most effective propaganda films of the Nazi regime, and won her a gold medal at the Venice Film Festival. When obligatory conscription was reintroduced in 1935, she shot another important propaganda film, *Tag der Freiheit: Unsere Wehrmach (Day of Freedom)*. She reached the high point of

BERTOLT BRECHT
Communist poet and playwright, whose works portray the human condition in a class-divided capitalist society, Brecht abandoned Germany after the Reichstag was burned down. He first sought refuge in Denmark, then moved to Hollywood in the United States where he lived in isolation for six years. After his inquisition by the Anti-American Activities Commission, he left America and lived out his final years in East Berlin.

emigrated. Many of those who stayed in Germany joined the so-called 'internal emigration', managing to carve out a tiny niche for themselves despite the strict censorship, and able to continue writing without toeing the line imposed from on high. Theatre, too, was subjugated to the Chamber of Culture after the great flourishing of the Weimar years. Productions propagandizing the new myths of the regime were given privileged treatment, but broad scope was also given to the more popular theatre of operetta and comedy which, despite being unaligned, was openly promoted as a means of entertaining the masses.

Figurative Art and Architecture

Targeting the avant-garde artistic production of the Weimar was one of the ways NSDAP aggressiveness manifested itself even before coming to power. After 1933, Goebbels declared his intention of reinstating the pure authentic values of a German form of art, and a figurative production was encouraged, culminating in the 1937 Munich exhibition. Traditional genres reigned supreme: portraits, still life, landscapes and images all had to transmit the supreme ideals of the new ideological conception of Nazism. Return to nature was idealized with bucolic country scenes, war was idealized with bellicose imagery, but most of all, the new Nazis were portrayed with their physical characteristics highlighted: blonde-haired, blue-eyed women and smiling, healthy children. At the same time, a violent, aggressive propaganda campaign was launched against so-called 'degenerate art', work produced by whoever did not adhere to these principles, and which was held up for public criticism in exhibitions set up in towns all over Germany; these were always well attended. Works by artists such as Klee and Kandinskij were featured. In

her career during the 1936 Olympic Games with *Olympia*, a film she took two years to produce; it was shown on the Führer's birthday in 1938 and it is still considered a masterpiece today. Leni Riefenstahl enjoyed great success during the Nazi era, but after the war denied having had any relationship with the Nazi élite. Accused in 1948 of exploiting 60 gypsies in one of her films by not paying them or doing anything to save them from being deported to Auschwitz, she was eventually acquitted, and a year later she successfully sued the illustrated magazine *Revue* for revealing the facts. A television documentary of 1982 brought the episode to the public eye again, but Riefenstahl chose to remain silent.

PICTURES AT AN EXHIBITION
Visitors at the exhibition of 'degenerate art' organized in Munich in 1937. Under this name, the Nazis included and banned masterpieces by artists such as Picasso, Van Gogh, Gaugin, Kandinskij, Grosz and painters from the Die Brücke group. The same fate befell the musician Arnold Schönberg, who was accused of having composed 'degenerate' music because he undermined traditional tonal values.

architecture, the state increased construction of representational buildings and motorways. Architecture played a leading role in self-representation and the exaltation of power because it was a direct or indirect means for promulgating the regime's ideology. This was evident in Albert Speer's ideas for rebuilding German towns, the plans displaying expressions of the rhetoric and monumentality of Nazi architecture: the immense spaces for the Nuremberg rallies and the unfinished plans to build the great Berlin that was to have become, in Hitler's ideal, the capital of the world, were the most eloquent testimony to Speer's work.

SCHOOLS AND UNIVERSITIES

Schools were fundamental for setting up the Nazi regime's cultural and propaganda machinery. Even more than places for education and socialization, they became places for militarization, as the youth organizations were. The nazification of teaching staff was swift, since few were wholly sympathetic to the republican cause. The economic crisis that had generated a perpetual climate of uncertainty contributed to fostering hatred of the republican government; while up to 1930 rejection of Weimar had manifested itself in non-adherence to the ideals of the republic, this later took the shape of active cooperation with Nazism. By the end of 1933, all teachers were 'racially pure' and faithful to the regime.

The new syllabuses were only prepared at the end of the 1930s; the real change was felt not so much in the organization of education as in a shift towards a greater ideological slant in everything that was taught. Racism was the underlying theme of every aspect of teaching, including mathematics and art. There were few new textbooks, their place mostly taken by pamphlets and short booklets which were

ERNST LUDWIG KIRCHNER, *NUDE LYING IN FRONT OF THE MIRROR* (1909–10)
Kirchner's canvases are dominated by issues of life and conflict in the metropolis, often crammed with glaringly coloured figures painted with tense brushstrokes.

ERICH HECKEL, *KG BRÜCKE* (1912)
Xylography by the expressionist artist, here in the form of an invitation to an exhibition by the movement in 1912. The works of Kirchner and Heckel were classified as 'degenerate art'.

THE 'UNIVERSAL METROPOLIS' View of the model of Germany along a north-south axis – the new capital designed by Albert Speer. Prominent are the triumphal arch and congress hall with its massive dome that would completely dwarf the Reichstag. The plan for the new 'universal metropolis' of the thousand-year-long Reich would have transformed the old urban make-up of Berlin.

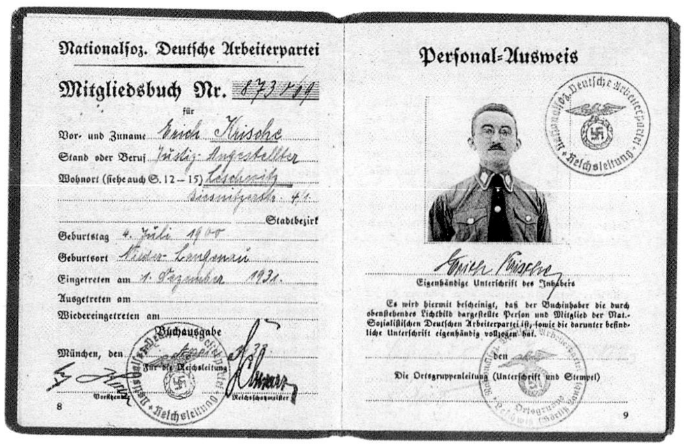

Nationalsoz. Deutsche Arbeiterpartei

Mitgliedsbuch Nr. 873 [illegible]

für

Vor- und Zuname Erich Krische

Stand oder Beruf Justiz-Angestellter

Wohnort (siehe auch S. 12–15) [illegible]

Stadtbezirk

Geburtstag 4. Juli 1900

Geburtsort [illegible]

Eingetreten am 1. Dezember 1931

Ausgetreten am

Wiedereingetreten am

München, den

Buchausgabe Für die Reichsleitung

Vorsitzender Reichsschatzmeister

8

Personal-Ausweis

Eigenhändige Unterschrift des Inhabers

Es wird hiermit bescheinigt, daß der Buchinhaber die durch obenstehendes Lichtbild dargestellte Person und Mitglied der Nat.-Sozialistischen Deutschen Arbeiterpartei ist, sowie die darunter befindliche Unterschrift eigenhändig vollzogen hat.

den

Die Ortsgruppenleitung (Unterschrift und Stempel)

9

Party Membership Card
Identity document for NSDAP members containing their name, occupation, address and date of birth. After being disbanded in 1923, the NSDAP was re-established two years later after deciding to renounce its clandestine struggle. It took its programme from *Mein Kampf* by Adolf Hitler, who in 1934 became undisputed leader of the party, the army and the state.

thought to be more to the point and easy to understand. As well as what was taught during the lessons, it was the everyday liturgy that marked daily life in school and developed the new Nazi values: the many occasions for celebrating important events, and the outings and the film screenings were opportunities for underlining the difference between who was 'Aryan' and who was not. It was even debated whether or not Jews were worthy of giving the Nazi salute that opened and closed every day at school.

Universities, on the other hand, were harder nuts to crack. While most of the professors were conservatives, and looked favourably on the new regime that promised to reinstate order after the chaos, it was harder to change what was already being taught and introduce new textbooks. The Nazi student organizations played a leading role in speeding up this levelling process; many young people were sure that the Third Reich would represent a new era in which they were going to play a crucial role.

The Party and the State

From June 1933 onwards, the NSDAP was the only legal political party in Germany. Hitler, who was the undisputed leader, skilfully managed to gather around himself élites, whose divergences stemmed not so much from differences in ideology (as happened with the Fascists in Italy) but from rivalry and power struggles which favoured and strengthened his own leadership.

In January 1933 there were 850,000 NSDAP members, the majority of whom were petty bourgeoisie, and approximately one-third blue-collar workers, half of whom were unemployed when the party took power. There were few women, but there were many more young people than in the

Labour Front at Nuremberg
The labour front replaced the disbanded trade unions and became the largest mass state organization of the Reich. It was supposed to ensure equality between entrepreneur and worker, but was actually rigidly hierarchical – grassroots members were obliged to bow down to the will of the leader (Führer) of the company.

ALBERT SPEER

Albert Speer was born into a family with liberal traditions in Mannheim in 1905. He followed in his father's footsteps by studying architecture and went to colleges in Karlsruhe, Munich and Berlin. Taken in by the skill of Hitler's oratory, he joined the NSDAP and the SA in 1931. From 1933, he was given the task of planning and organizing the choreography of the regime's mass rallies. His organizational skill and ability was appreciated by Hitler, who entrusted him with the task of designing the new chancellery in Berlin and the areas in Nuremberg where the party congresses were to be held. In 1937 he was appointed Inspector General for building in Berlin, and in 1938 he was given the title of professor, appointed to the Prussian State Council, and was awarded a senior Nazi Party decoration. Also in 1938, he became director of the office that responded to the German labour front. In 1942, his career reached a turning point. After the death of Fritz Todt, Speer rose to the position of Minister for Armaments and Supplies (from 1943 renamed Minister for Armaments and War Production) and was also appointed Inspector General for road transport, water resources and energy. Speer turned his efforts to transforming the arms industry so that it was totally geared to war production, and despite the heavy damage Allied bombing caused to the infrastructure and to the supplies of raw materials that fuelled the German economy, he achieved considerable success. The fact that industrial output reached its highest point in 1944 was due to Speer's exploitation of slave labour provided by the concentration camp detainees and foreign workers. In this project, Speer worked alongside Oswald Pohl and Fritz Sauckel, both condemned to death at the Nuremberg trials. At Nuremberg, Speer maintained that he did not realize the Axis powers had lost the war until the beginning of 1945 and that he had no idea of the plan to exterminate the Jews. As a result, he was only given a 20-year jail sentence for crimes against humanity. In the years he spent imprisoned at Spandau, he wrote *Inside the Third Reich*, which, despite its many omissions, remains a useful insight into the history of the Nazi regime. Freed in October 1966, he died in London in 1981.

ACADEMY OF GYMNASTICS AND THE NEW CHANCELLERY IN BERLIN (Centre page)
Inspired by the ideals of true classicism, the new Reich chancellery designed by Speer was an example of architecture which, although slanted towards functionality, was measured by its grandiosity. Using 4,500 workers in two shifts, it was built in less than a year.

SPEER WITH HITLER (Left)

LIGHTING FOR THE OLYMPICS
View of a Berlin square during the Olympic games.

SCULPTURES NEAR THE BRANDENBURG GATE
(Below)

bourgeois parties or in the Social Democrats. After 30 January, membership grew sharply – especially teachers and white-collar workers – to the point where the party's numbers had tripled by May of that year. The borderline between state and party grew increasingly blurred until a law of 1 December 1933 confirmed that they were one and the same. The NSDAP essentially became a public corporation, the Führer's closest aide and the SA's head of armed forces both became members of the government, and the party won the right to try its members by special laws that were outside ordinary law.

The tendency of identifying state and party allowed the latter to enjoy a lesser or greater degree of independence depending on what the tactics of the occasion called for. This institutional co-penetration stood out clearly in the case of the *Gauleiters*, those in charge of the regions, who combined the functions of party members and state bureaucrats: a number of them were even ministers (such as Goebbels), while many held other posts in public administration. Alongside the regional heads of the Nazi party, there were all the other party organizations: the SS, the *Hitlerjugend*, the student bodies and women's associations, by means of which the NSDAP exercised one of its most fundamental functions – educating the nation and selecting those who would take on roles of responsibility within the state.

SPORT AND OLYMPICS

Sport – particularly in the sense of physical movement, competition and the strengthening of assertiveness – was considered fundamental to the new German man. Sports associations – blue-collar worker, religious and party – had developed considerably in the 1920s, in particular among young people. From 1933 onwards, the 'levelling out' process taking place in politics was enacted in sport too. Worker-party sport associations were disbanded and their assets taken over by police 'trustees'.

On 10 May 1933, the Reich sports organization was set up, and it subjected all other sports associations to strict control by the central power. All their members had to declare allegiance to the central organization and observe its rules and regulations. Sports activities of a clearly warlike nature became increasingly practised even in schools; young people had to face challenges of hardiness, and long marches in preparation for the far more arduous battles they would have to undertake when fighting for their country. In preparation for war, physical activity also became increasingly important in the *Hitlerjugend*. As had been decided in 1931, the 1936 Olympics were to be held in Berlin, despite the racist nature of the Nazi Party being irreconcilable with the cosmopolitan character of the games. In 1935, the International Olympic Committee expressed objections, especially regarding the Nazi ban on Jewish athletes; Goebbels provided the committee with answers as vague as they were reassuring, but they were ultimately deemed satisfactory. The NSDAP, initially against holding the games in Germany, changed its mind after understanding what a unique opportunity this was for staging a grandiose propaganda parade in a period so delicate for Nazi foreign policy. The Berlin games presented the ideal opportunity for putting on a façade to show athletes and journalists a seemingly 'normal' country. During the competitions, the harsher, more anti-Semitic outbursts of the regime's propaganda were toned down and a semblance of order and efficiency was imposed which completely fooled the foreign press (who were all in agreement on how genuine the Olympic games had been).

POSTER FOR THE 1936 WINTER OLYMPICS
(Above)

MEDAL AWARDED TO THE ORGANIZERS OF THE GAMES

GOTTFRIED VON CRAMM
Von Cramm was a successful German tennis champion in the 1930s. (Left)

Economic policy

The seriousness of the repercussions of the 1929 crash was one of the factors that brought the NSDAP to power – its promises to do away with unemployment were attractive to the German electorate. The 'socialism' the party evoked in its name turned out to be a demagogic idea behind which lurked the policy of creating a hierarchical structure in the workplace. The NSDAP's manifesto pledged to be sympathetic to the middle classes, but this turned out to be a hollow promise. Gottfried Feder, who had spread the slogan of the 'end of debt slavery', was moved away from the Ministry of Economy in 1934, thus muzzling the anti-capitalist faction that had played such an important role in the party's early years. Beyond exalting farm workers as the 'source of life' of the new Aryan race, the regime's agricultural policy made no structural changes, leaving the power of the big landowners unchallenged and making no improvements in the conditions for farm workers.

Working on the Motorway
The beginnings of the building of the German motorway network.
(Page 64)

Handshake
Hitler with a group of workers.
(Page 65)

German Savers

The Aeronautical Engineer Willy Messerschmitt and the Krupp Factory at Essen.
(Below)

Nazi economic policy was aimed at rearmament and preparation for war, and this gained momentum in 1934 when the four-year plan became law. German industry, internally split and with objectives that were in part contradictory, was far from eager to grant top priority to rearmament. However, the eradication of the country's political left, the freedom of scope granted to industry and the new climate of police terror, all laid the foundations for cooperation between the Nazi government and large-scale industry, which instigated a job creation programme that stimulated the economy and began to reap the benefits of the booming war economy.

The First Measures

By 1933, Germany was the only European country that had begun to recover from the world economic slump. This was made possible by a long-term economic trend that gained momentum a year later through policies aiming towards economic self-sufficiency and the impetus given to war production by massive orders placed by the state.

In order to generate the necessary credit, Hjalmar Schacht, president of the Reich Bank and Minister of Finance from August 1934, set up a company with one million marks of capital put up by the owners of heavy industry companies such as Krupps and Siemens. Taxable notes for a total of 12 billion marks were issued which could be paid from 1938. In order to make these viable, more paper money was printed than the state was able to guarantee, and the funding of arms

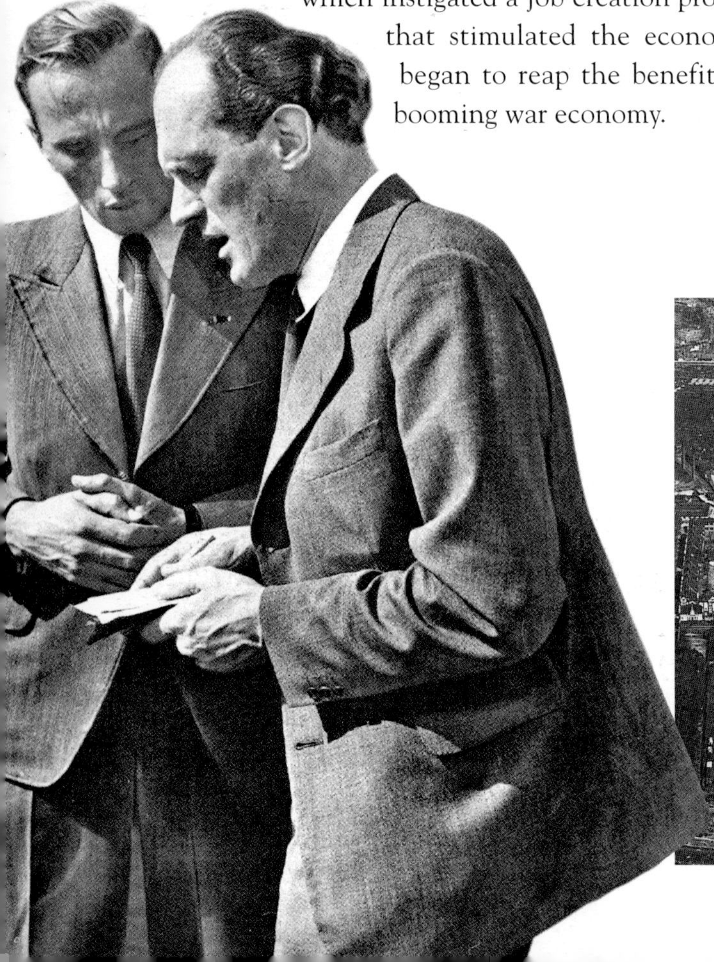

MERCEDES-BENZ MOTOR VEHICLES
Advertising poster for the car manufacturer.

FAMILY PORTRAIT
The arms industry magnate Gustav Krupp (standing, right) portrayed with his wife (seated, right) and family in a painting from 1931. (Below)

manufacture and full employment rode on the back of inflationary policies; the state pinned its hopes of paying its debts on the future profits derived from winning the war. Germany's economic development was clearly reflected in its military expenditure, which was impossible to finance solely by taxes. Indeed, the amount spent on the military rose from 4 per cent of public expenditure in 1933 to 18 per cent in 1934, and then shot up to 50 per cent in 1938.

Major industry increasingly sided with the new regime as can be seen, for example, in the donations to Adolf Hitler that financed the 1933 election campaign; after an appeal by Gustav Krupp, these later turned into an annual donation that was equal to 5 per cent of German companies' total wage bill for 1932.

The first example of state intervention without nationalizing the economy occurred at the end of 1933 with the establishment of the IG Farben cartel for the creation of new factories to produce synthetic fuel. The idea was that synthetic fuel production would guarantee German economic self-sufficiency, and on 1 December 1934 a law was passed to create economic benefits for the construction of new factories for the production of petrol, Buna and cellulose wool.

In foreign trade, Schacht put forward a new plan, what he called the 'German New Deal'. This would boost trade, especially with central-eastern Europe, and was intended to address the problem of the country's lack of raw materials.

Against such massive investment in rearmament, money

'Intellectual and manual workers Elect Soldier Hitler!'
Nazi electoral poster.

spent on social policies was by comparison very small. Housing, for example, was much worse than during the Weimar years, and measures such as the subventions provided for in the regime's matrimonial policies were paid for by cutting the funding of other social issues. The Reich's debt rose from 12.9 billion marks in 1933 to 31 billion in 1938. Currency stability and social peace were at risk, but the decision to rearm quickly was not going to be reversed and was given top priority over everything else.

Combating Unemployment

Reinstating full employment in Germany was a constant promise made by the Nazi propaganda machine. It was achieved both through a general economic upturn and by the introduction of a number of effective measures. Schacht implemented a policy of deficit spending that was unusual for the times; by spurring economic growth it created massive state debt. The laws combating unemployment put this principle into practice and granted credits to regions and municipalities which, in turn, launched a series of public works such as the building of motorways – using as little machinery as possible to increase the manpower involved. Part of the success of these projects was that one condition for receiving credits was that women couldn't work; if they did, they had to hand their jobs over to their husbands.

Not only did this cut male unemployment, but it also spurred demographic growth as women now had time to dedicate themselves exclusively to the role of motherhood. From 1935, the reintroduction of obligatory conscription, plus six months of enforced labour for all males between 18 and 25, took even more pressure off the labour market. Anyone involved in 'labour service' and young people doing farm

***Die Internationale* (*The International*) by Otto Griebel (1930)**
(Below)

CHARLES LINDBERGH
The American aviator pictured during a visit to a German airfield in the mid-1930s.

work on a fixed-term basis, did not count as being unemployed. The destruction of the trade unions combined with the new hierarchical organization within factories made it easier for the authorities to control the labour market.

Apart from all this, there was a genuine drop in unemployment. When Hitler came to power there were some five million out of work, but in 1935 that figure had dropped to little over two million; the year after that, some industries, such as building and metal-working, were complaining about the lack of available labour.

The success of the employment policy depended on the economy being tied to war production and was achieved at the price of completely abolishing working-class autonomy. However, after the difficult period of the economic slump, many Germans felt that having a permanent job was much more important.

AGRICULTURAL POLICY

Nazi propaganda had emphasized the importance of agriculture and the world of the farm worker, which lay at the heart of German racial purity. Walter Darré, Minister of Agriculture and head of the farmers' corporation, was the main architect of agrarian reform. He launched the *Reichsnährstand* (Reich foodstuffs corporation) to which all farmers who traded in or were involved in the industrial processing of farm produce belonged; all previous agricultural associations and organizations were disbanded. The new officials, however, did not always manage to gain the upper hand, as witnessed, for example, in the close links between many farmers and the Jewish traders who often provided needed credit. A consequence of the new policy was that farmers lost all independence.

In point of fact, public intervention only covered technical matters and left the chemical industry cartels and

WALTER DARRÉ

Born into an Argentinian trading family in 1895, Darré moved to Germany and volunteered to serve in World War I. Following the war, he studied agrarian economics and was appointed to state jobs in animal breeding. In 1929, he published *Das Bauerntum als Lebensquell der Nordischen Rasse* (*The Peasantry as the Life Source of the Nordic Race*), and in 1930 *Neuadel aus Blut und Boden* (*New Aristocracy from Blood and Soil*). These works developed his idea that the German people had to undergo racial renewal, which could only take place by returning to the countryside and abandoning industrial development. Darré joined the NSDAP in 1930 and from the beginning forged a strong relationship with Himmler and Hitler. Up to the point when they took power, he was an ardent campaigner for the party and was particularly attentive to cultivating links with farm workers, setting up a monthly publication for them in 1932. He worked

closely with Himmler in defining racial standards which were to become a feature of the SS. After the NSDAP took power, he became head of its agricultural policy, and then Minister for Agriculture. When the four-year plan became law in 1936, his influence diminished, and continued to do so through the war years. Jailed in 1945, he was sentenced to seven years imprisonment in 1949, but was pardoned the following year. He died in Munich in 1953.

Work Service Awards Given Out by the Reich in 1934

Kraft Durch Freude
A farm in a poster for the Nazi labour organization. (Below, left)

Peasant Women in Traditional Costume
The agricultural policy of the Reich was unable to stem the haemorrhage of people from the countryside. (Below, right)

major landowners free to set unjust working conditions and fix the prices of farm produce. There was no reform of the landowning situation because support from the major landowners had always underpinned Nazi power and would continue to do so. A law passed in September 1933, which tied the first-born son to properties of up to 125 hectares – making them indivisible and inalienable – underlined the subjugation of farmers to the land and deprived them of any chance of changing their lot. It was true that the law forbade mortgages to be raised on that land, thus protecting those with debts, but lack of capital made further investment impossible. Apart from the propaganda rhetoric, the regime's agricultural policies brought no perceptible benefits; on the contrary, the countryside was progressively abandoned over the years – but despite this Germany reached 80 per cent of agricultural self-sufficiency.

The Working Class

Blue-collar workers and their political and trade union organizations and associations were the first targets of Nazi attacks, and already in 1933 nothing was left of the broad, multi-faceted array of groups and structures of the Weimar years. Blue-collar workers were regimented to speed up productivity without the means of making claims or demonstrating discontent. The German labour front, headed by Robert Ley, was set up in May which, with over 25 million members, became the Nazis' largest mass organization. Ley's idea was for it to penetrate every area of German economic life. A sounding board for the regime's social policies, and with far-reaching mechanisms for applying conformity, it was one of the regime's most effective tools for infiltrating society at grass-roots level and applying psychological pressure on the working masses. The vast amount of money the front

CRUISES FOR THE WORKERS
The poster proclaims: 'Now you, too, can travel!' Organized trips for blue- and white-collar workers and their families created the illusion that the poorer classes could enjoy the same pleasures as the bourgeoisie.

collected from membership contributions was used to maintain an elephantine structure of bureaucrats.

The typical blurring of party and state that marked the Third Reich was much in evidence here. The NSDAP ran the labour front, monitoring the political and social trustworthiness of its members on behalf of the state, in particular extending its presence to beyond working hours by deciding how free time was to be spent. This task was undertaken by the *Kraft Durch Freude* (Strength Through Joy) organization which launched a whole series of events, from theatre visits to concerts, short trips to cultural activities. Although the activities were relatively cheap, more white-collar workers took advantage of them than blue-collar and many used them to escape from their daily routine.

The idea behind these events was to exalt the nationalist aspect of the collective spirit in order to create at least a momentary illusion that above and beyond the class struggle, it was possible to belong to the *Volksgemeinschaft* (community of people). In reality, it was far from egalitarian, and actually very hierarchical.

THE ORGANIZATION OF LABOUR

In the course of 1934, a number of measures were introduced which defined the new economic and social order. A law governing national labour was passed on 20 January 1934, ensuring that every factory had a rigid hierarchical structure: entrepreneurs were the bosses, and white-and blue-collar workers had to obey them blindly 'in order to promote the interests of the company and the common good of the people and the state'. Trade unionists were replaced by trustees – appointed by industrialists and Nazi organizations – who kept order and discipline on a tight rein. In May of 1934, a law was passed

ROBERT LEY

Ley was born in 1890 into a well-to-do farm-working family. He volunteered for World War I and was seriously wounded in 1917. He joined the NSDAP in 1925 and rose to become the party leader for South Rhineland. He was sacked by Bayer for his violent anti-Semitic attacks against the Jewish banker, Warburg, who was on the company's board of directors. He was elected to the Reichstag in 1930, and rose to become head of the Committee of Action for the Protection of the German Worker in 1932 and, after the party came to power, was responsible for the destruction of trade union associations and their offices. As head of the labour front, which was set up and funded by the assets that were confiscated from the Weimar Republic's workers' organizations, Ley held a post of senior responsibility in the Reich. He also established the 'Adolf Hitler' schools for the sons of the party. Arrested just before the end of the war by the American army, he was due to be tried at Nuremberg; however, he committed suicide in prison.

THE LEADER OF THE LABOUR FRONT IS PICTURED BETWEEN SPEER AND GOEBBELS

Fritz Todt
Todt was the engineer who designed the German motorway system and the West Wall; he was Minister of Armaments from 1940 to 1942, when he was killed in an aircraft accident.

The Nazi, 1 May
Poster for the first celebration of the 'National Festival of Work', it was renamed to eradicate any class connotation.

Rally of the Labour Front
(Below)

regulating worker placement. In 1935, the introduction of the 'labour book' made worker mobility even more difficult. That same year, an obligatory six-month 'work service' was introduced for youths aged from 18 to 25. Besides taking pressure off the labour market, it served the important function of imposing political conformity, selection and discipline.

The regime's desire to weaken the workers' class-based ideas gained momentum not only from the introduction of a far-reaching set of repressive measures, but also through working conditions. Employees were forced to work for unbearable numbers of hours as production became increasingly focused on the war effort; the introduction of piecework unleashed competitiveness among workers that broke with the idea of class solidarity. The working class became increasingly divided, split by contrasts and bereft of its contractual power despite there being no lack of episodes – especially in industries where full employment had been achieved – of workers aware of their importance and winning wage increases. This was sometimes due to the mediation of the labour front, whose supposed function as an intermediary was always somewhat ambiguous.

The Four-Year Plan

At the 1936 Nuremberg rally, the four-year plan was announced, a move to prepare the whole economic system for the prospect of war. At the rally, Hitler declared: 'Within four years Germany must reach full independence from abroad in all raw materials that can be produced by German skill, by our chemistry, our mechanical industries as well as from our mines.' There was now no relationship between expenditure and profits: economic self-sufficiency had to be reached in time for the new war. Hermann Göring was placed

FACTORY WORKERS With Nazism, inflation and unemployment ceased, but the price the German working class had to pay for stability and full employment was iron-fisted regimentation in the factory, discipline in the workplace, as well as the suppression of the freedom to associate and the right to negotiate pay and working conditions.

HJALMAR SCHACHT

Schacht was born in 1877 into a family of traders. He studied economics and then began a brilliant career in banking. In 1918, he was one of the founder members of the liberal, progressive German Democratic Party. In 1923, he started becoming active in Weimar economic policies, and made contributions to reducing the country's rampant inflation. That same year he was appointed governor of the Reichsbank. Disagreement with the government's financial policies led him to resign in 1930, and he began frequenting more conservative circles. In March 1933, Hitler re-appointed him Reichsbank governor and the following year he became Minister of Economy. In May 1935, he was given full powers for the war economy, which caused friction between him and Göring. In November 1937, he left his ministerial posts and in 1939 resigned from the bank governorship. Up to 1943, he was a minister without portfolio with no influence at all. He left politics before war broke out and the German economy collapsed, but he had been partly responsible for that situation, having greatly benefited from the risks the regime's economic and political choices had brought. Schacht was arrested in 1944 because of the contacts he had established with the opposition movement that had organized the 20 July assassination attempt, and was imprisoned in the camps of Ravensbrück and Flossenburg. Deferred to the Nuremberg tribunal for his part in German re-armament, he was acquitted. Later, a court in Stuttgart sentenced him to eight years forced labour, but he served only one year. In the 1950s, he began another brilliant career as economic and financial adviser to developing countries. He died in Munich in 1970.

SCHACHT PHOTOGRAPHED IN THE 1920S

DURING A PAUSE IN THE NUREMBERG TRIALS
Schacht having a meal in the company of other detainees, including von Papen (to his left).

Synthetic Rubber Produced in the IG Farben Factory

Hitler Visiting the Berlin Auto Exhibition
(Below)

in charge of the four-year plan and was empowered to pass every legal and administrative measure necessary which, hierarchically, placed him above all the heads of the economic ministry. The best results in achieving productive self-sufficiency came from the chemical industry.

From the point of view of the organization of the economic structure, the plan made no sweeping changes; the state did not play a direct role in managing the economy, but it did keep a number of coordinating tasks aside for itself. The only direct action taken was to create a number of state enterprises, among the most important of which was the Hermann Göring Works, a large company for working iron-based minerals and developing metallurgy. After the four-year plan was proclaimed, no significant changes were introduced into the economic system save for a number of transformations within the monopolistic system, although it was no coincidence that the biggest concentration took place in the key sectors of chemistry and mining.

HERMANN GÖRING

Göring was born near Rosenheim, in Bavaria, in 1893. His father was a career diplomat and at the time was consul-general in Haiti. Göring decided to follow a military career and by 1914 had risen to the rank of infantry lieutenant. When war broke out, he enrolled in the air force and fought as a fighter pilot, winning the highest award, the *Ordre Pour le Mérite*. He met Hitler in 1922 and joined the NSDAP, becoming head of the newly created SA organization. He took part in the Munich Putsch, and when it failed he fled to Sweden – his wife's country of origin. He returned to Germany in 1927 in the wake of a political amnesty. In 1928 he was elected to the Reichstag and rose to its presidency after the NSDAP won the 1932 elections. His fame as a World War I hero and his contacts among the economically influential, the army and the aristocracy all contributed to him playing a crucial role in the rise of Nazism. After the regime came to power, Göring was highly influential in creating its image of terror. He was Prussian Interior Minister and Chief of Police as well as being minister without portfolio in Hitler's first government. In May 1933 he became head of aeronautics, from which the future Luftwaffe would emerge. He strengthened his position in 1934 as Hitler's deputy, to the point that a law passed in December secretly appointed him successor to the Führer. In 1936, he was made responsible for implementing the four-year plan, and it was from this position that he laid the basis for his growing political influence during a period when the Reich was aiming to go to war to acquire *Lebensraum*. When war broke out, Göring was at the very height of his power, but it was then that he began to lose prestige and political influence. He was sentenced to death at Nuremberg, but committed suicide shortly before his execution took place.

In Soldier's Uniform
On Göring's return from Sweden, Hitler gave him the task of winning over the large German middle-class to the cause of Nazism.

Wearing a Leather Jacket and Gilded Dagger
Göring's star waned during the long drawn-out battle for Stalingrad when the Luftwaffe was unable to guarantee safe passage for supplies vital to von Paulus' VI Division, which was worn out by the rigours of battle and the extreme cold of the long Russian winter.

Berlin Department Store

Politics and Economics

The merging of the aims of the Nazi leadership and those of German capitalism grew closer as the years passed. The state and the leading sectors of industry blended even more closely than before so that after war broke out, the drive, responsibility and administrative control of the economy passed into private hands, and those in charge held enormous sway over the political and military decisions that affected the economy. The boundaries between the state's economic administration and the private economy became increasingly blurred. The alliance between the military-industrial complex and the Nazi ruling élite, which had been forged during rearmament and the expansionist programme, lasted until the dying days of the Third Reich. It is also true, however, that the balance of power in this alliance shifted progressively towards the Nazi leadership, and in the crucial moments of the history of the Third Reich, the political and ideological demands of the Nazi leaders became ever more important when it came to making political decisions.

From 1936, the internal redistribution of power began: when the four-year plan became law, there was a sharp fall in the direct influence of industry in political decisions. From then on, ideological considerations were more important in making decisions and setting political priorities. German industry made enormous gains both through the regime's process of 'Aryanization' and its territorial expansionism. This impetus, however, shifted increasingly towards high-risk policies featuring a faster arms race and narrower margins for major economic interests to manoeuvre in. Private industry was crucial to rearmament, and it was this that enabled those within it to maintain considerable power of negotiation during the Third Reich. The introduction of the four-

Music for the Workers
A concert by the Vienna Philharmonic, conducted by Wilhelm Furtwängler, held in a German factory.

'AT FIVE MARKS A WEEK YOU, TOO, CAN OWN A CAR!'
So reads the advert for the 'people's car'. It was Hitler's idea to produce a vehicle that would extend the benefits of car use to broad sectors of German society.

year plan in 1936 produced a wartime economy, even though Germany was not yet at war. Richard Darré, President of the German Agricultural Society, announced the 'battle for food' policy in an attempt to make the nation self-sufficient. Since Germany lacked many of the core materials required to make weapons the Nazi government refocused German imports away from consumer goods and towards the objective of rearmament. To fund the rearmament drive, taxes were kept at the high levels introduced during the recession. Although by 1938 German's food production had increased by 20% since 1928, the average citizen was only consuming 5% more calories than in 1932, the worst year of the depression. The money the government was spending on imports was unsustainable; although Hitler had planned for war, he had spent so much on rearmament that by 1939 he had no option other than to invade Poland to finance further weapons production.

During the war, economic factors remained inextricably linked to ideology and strategic and military considerations in deciding how developing the German offensive. The continuing problems of the availability and assignation of raw materials and the workforce enabled the heads of the main industries of the war effort to maintain a considerable say in political decisions. An imperialist war of pillage became the only possible alternative and German industry became an accessory to the decisions that were to lead towards a level of destruction and inhumanity never before seen in European history.

Up to the end of the war, every sector of finance and industry linked to the production of armaments received enormous benefits from the Reich. In 1939, profits not paid out by limited companies were four times higher than in 1928. Those who held a monopoly, first and foremost the chemical giant IG Farben, made the biggest gains.

BUILDING WAR PLANES
Within the rearmament programme, the state offered generous support to heavy industry. (Below)

THE BEETLE

Hitler supported Ferdinand Porsche's plan to build a 'car for the people' as a propaganda exercise and to encourage car use in Germany. But because the car manufacturer that was to have built the new model gave an indirect thumbs-down to the idea, the eventual company that produced the Volkswagen built its own factory at Wolfsburg along with the labour front. Here, in accordance with the will of the Führer, a model worker's city was built on a plan developed by the architect Peter Koller; a place where industry, leisure time and living space were closely linked, with party offices and buildings in the city centre.

The car made its debut in September 1938, but not a single car was delivered to any of the 336,000 people who had already ordered one nor to any of the 66,000 who had paid for one in full because, with the war on, the new company had to switch its production to support the war effort.

PRESENTATION OF THE BEETLE
The few models actually produced went exclusively to SS officials and members of the Nazi élite.

FERDINAND PORSCHE (Left)

NAZI KULTUR
ALBERT EINSTEIN
LEON TROTSKY
V.I. LENIN
FRANZ BOAS

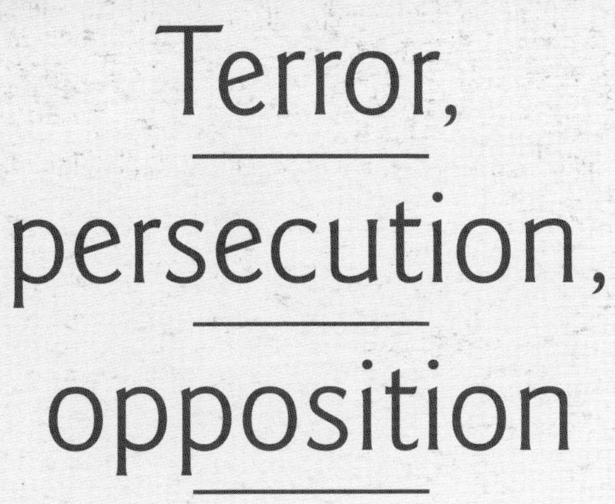

Terror, persecution, opposition

The instrument used by the Nazi Party to carry out the Führer's will and to guarantee order was the police. Although it was the only state institution empowered to use force, it acted much more in the interests of the party than of the state. Indeed, the way the police force was structured showed the extent to which state and party had been unified. Immediately after the Nazis' rise to power, Hermann Göring, Minister of Internal Affairs for Prussia, carried out a radical reorganization of the internal security services, creating a secret state police force – the Gestapo. Political police were also set up in all the other *Länder* (regions). In Bavaria, Heinrich Himmler, head of the SS since 1929, was in charge; his chief aide was Reinhard Heydrich, who in 1931 created the *Sicherheitsdienst* (security service), a powerful instrument of control over both opposition parties and organizations and over unruly elements within the Nazi Party. After the elimination of the SA in 1934, Himmler's power grew

HITLER IN A FRESCO BY THE MEXICAN ARTIST DIEGO RIVERA (1933)
(Page 80)

FLOWERS FOR THE FÜHRER
Hitler's image was worshipped in many German homes. (Page 81)

ID BADGE OF THE STATE SECRET POLICE (GESTAPO)

enormously, and all the political police, except in Prussia, were united under his command.

In June 1936, Hitler issued a decree to regulate this cumbersome apparatus and make it more centralized. He placed it under the command of Himmler, who in theory responded to the Minister of the Interior, but in reality acted independently. In the union between state and political police, the SS was by far the most powerful element, so much so that Himmler did not even have an office in the Ministry of the Interior. In 1936, the police were divided into two forces, one for order and the other for security, with Heydrich in control of the latter.

THE ADMINISTRATION OF JUSTICE

Under the Nazi regime, the law became a means for persecuting enemies and undesirables. After Hitler came to power, there were no major changes in the Ministry of Justice since the majority of its staff were politically conservative anyway and willing to follow the new government's orders. Jews were dismissed and, after 1935, women could no longer serve as judges. On an administrative level, the end of local autonomy meant that the ministry was now in sole charge of a truty vast system which until that time had been largely decentralized.

The changes were applied to areas outside the administrative structure: broad jurisdictional autonomy was created for the SA and then for the SS, and many aspects of the law were amended – especially private law. After the burning of the Reichstag, the death penalty was brought back for certain crimes. An ever-growing number of sectors were subtracted from ordinary justice and assigned to special tribunals. Whereas the special tribunal for political crimes and the

HEINRICH HIMMLER

Born in Munich in 1900 into a strict, staunchly monarchist Catholic family, Himmler took part in the 1923 Munich Putsch with Hitler. He joined the NSDAP in 1925 along with Gregor Strasser, and that same year became substitute *Gauleiter* (leader) for southern Bavaria; from 1926 to 1930, he was appointed substitute chief of propaganda. In 1929, he was named head of the SS and the year after elected to the Reichstag. As Munich Chief of Police in 1933, he opened the concentration camp at Dachau which was destined to become the model for all other camps. He was one of the most enthusiastic organizers of the massacre of Röhm and the SA in 1934. In the years to follow, his career grew as the power of the SS increased; he was one of the most powerful members of the regime's political apparatus. Although he was never

REINHARD HEYDRICH
A member of the SS since 1931, Heydrich played a leading role in the 'night of the long knives', in anti-Jewish violence that culminated in the 'night of the broken glass' and in planning the extermination of Europe's Jews. (Left)

WILHELM FRICK
Reich Minister of the Interior from 1933 to 1943 and then Reichsprotektor of Bohemia-Moravia, Frick was sentenced to death at Nuremberg.

popular court of justice were still looked after by the Minister of Justice, the new tribunals of the Wehrmacht were autonomous, and after 1938 had the authority to judge civilians under certain circumstances. It was on this model that in 1934 Heinrich Himmler founded an honour tribunal for the SS. Changes were also made in family law: marriages could be prohibited on the grounds of safeguarding racial purity and mixed couples were encouraged to separate.

The Nazi concept of law was no longer based on guaranteeing the rights of the individual and the equality of everyone before the law; rather, it gave priority to the interests of the community and the obligation for people to serve it. Many new punishments were applied retroactively and, in general, they grew much harsher, as can be seen in the exponential growth in the number of those sentenced to death, especially after the outbreak of war.

CONSENSUS AND SILENCE

Contrary to what Nazi propaganda wanted to portray, German society did not wholeheartedly support the regime. The enthusiasm was only a façade, and after national socialism came to power, it was marked by personal jostling for power and the shallow rituals of parades. The masses, who couldn't care less about politics, slumped into a passive state of malcontent, with everyone coming to terms with the regime.

There were, however, many aspects of Nazi policy that met with widespread favour. Most important was its successful foreign policy: the fact

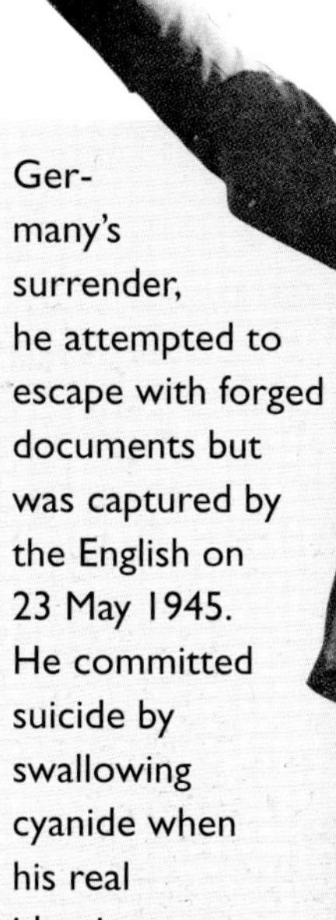

well liked by the reigning élite, he was feared for the maniacal attention he gave to everything in his charge. He dedicated himself to the tutelage of the 'Aryan race', particularly by creating the élite caste of the SS and the foundation of the '*Lebensborn*'. After the outbreak of war, he was one of those most responsible for organizing the extermination of the Jews by the *Einstazgruppen* (Special Action Groups) in territories occupied by the Wehrmacht, the ghettos, and the death camps. He was also responsible for the Germanization of the annexed territories and as such was one of the main strategists of 'total war' in the East. In the spring of 1945, he was shorn of all his responsibilities and thrown out of the Nazi Party when he declared himself in favour of a partial surrender – Himmler believed that it would be possible to continue fighting against the USSR alongside the western powers. Immediately after Germany's surrender, he attempted to escape with forged documents but was captured by the English on 23 May 1945. He committed suicide by swallowing cyanide when his real identity was discovered.

ONLY HITLER
This pronouncement by Baldur von Schirach was testimony of the cult surrounding the Führer: 'Adolf Hitler, we believe in you. Without you we would be single individuals. Through you we are a people. It is you who gives purpose to our youth.'

HITLER TAKING THE SALUTE IN NUREMBERG 1934 (Below)

that in such a short time Hitler was able to overturn the discriminatory clauses of the Treaty of Versailles and to win age-old territorial claims (such as the unification of all Germans in one great Germany) was received with genuine enthusiasm by a vast majority of the population. What counted for many Germans was not only the results achieved, but also the methods employed: after a decade of hesitant and contradictory foreign policy, mostly characterized by a readiness to compromise, Hitler gave the German people the impression that his strategy, although risky, had led to notable successes. Many Germans saw the regime's economic and social legislative measures in a similar light. It seemed as though the new regime had achieved a radical turnaround – after years of insecurity and unemployment, satisfying the basic needs of food and work was by and large guaranteed from about 1936. The policy of terror also found widespread favour when it promised to establish 'order', even if this involved the persecution of the opposition and the violent suppression of the smallest form of dissent. The fact that it was possible to leave an unlocked bicycle in front of a house without anyone stealing it, or that there were no 'deviants' roaming the streets, was considered a great achievement of the regime. All this enhanced the myth of the immense superiority of the Führer, who was given credit for every success. This myth constituted a potent force for the creation of mass consensus.

ORDER AND TERROR

The favour that wide sectors of the population accorded particular aspects of Nazi policy did, however, somehow involve it in the policy of terror, above and beyond a mere passive acceptance. After 1933, Hitler came out against all forms of spontaneous brown-shirt terrorism, and the murder of Röhm

THE SA

The SA (*Sturmabteilung*, storm troopers) was founded by the Nazi Party in 1920 to act as a police force to safeguard the party's initiatives and to constitute a strong assault force for street violence. It had roughly 300 members in 1921; by 1933, there were over 400,000. Ernst Röhm turned it into a paramilitary organization, but he quit the party in 1925 because of growing conflicts with Hitler. Röhm became leader of the SA again in 1931, appointed by Hitler himself, and kept this position until his murder in 1934. The brown-shirts conducted their politics mainly in the streets, attempting to attract supporting crowds in the towns and in working-class neighbourhoods, and hoping to entice the young in particular to join them. Their tactics were based on provocation and violence, creating a spiral of ever-growing aggression that many members of the party wanted to stop. After the Nazis came to power, Göring signed a decree allowing the SA to open prisons, run concentration camps and make arrests. Among the most infamous of its initiatives came on 1 April 1933, when it called on people to boycott Jewish shops. That same year, the confused and contradictory political situation found many members of the SA holding public offices that by then had to be incorporated in the Nazi state. Hitler's plans no longer included the 'second revolution' called for by the SA, hence his decision to massacre Röhm and other SA members in the 'night of the long knives'. In the years to follow, the activities of the SA focused on pre-military training of youths and street demonstrations.

Its propensity for terrorism, never really suppressed, re-emerged in all its barbarity in the 'night of the broken glass' (9 November 1938), when many Jews were killed and the synagogues, homes and shops of German Jews were set on fire.

'FORWARD, SA!'
Poster showing a menacing brown-shirt.

RALLY OF ASSAULT GROUPS IN 1920

THE SS

The SS (*Schutzstaffeln*, protection squads) was founded in 1925 as Hitler's bodyguard unit. At first it was under the command of the head of the SA, and in theory this remained unchanged even when Himmler took over as its chief in 1929. Himmler, however, tried to promote the idea that the corps should be the élite of the National Socialist movement, with close ties to the Führer (as can be seen in the slogan 'Member of the SS, your honour is called fidelity'). Providing a service as informers under Reinhard Heydrich, the SS increasingly took on the role of Nazi Party police. After the Nazis came to power, the role of Himmler remained stable, but the following year his position changed significantly when he became chief of the political police for the whole of Germany. He was supported by Wilhelm Frick, Minister of Internal Affairs, who wanted to get rid of regional divisions in the police force. Göring, President of Prussian Ministers, looked favourably on this broadening of Himmler's power, since he had every interest in weakening the SA.

After the 'night of the long knives', the power of the SS became even greater. Its members, who by the end of the 1920s numbered no more than a few hundred men, had by 1933 become an army of over 50,000, and were destined in part to take on the role of the police, and in part to evolve into a volunteer army of political soldiers for the NSDAP.

The SS ran the terrorist apparatus of the regime, taking over direct control of the concentration and death camps, which was trusted to special divisions (called 'death heads'). A privileged caste tied to Himmler and Hitler by an oath that highlighted its fanatical character, the SS was considered by Himmler to be the source of Aryan purity. The outbreak of war only heightened this role, since its main function was the Germanization of all the occupied territories.

Himmler with Top-ranking Officers of the SS in Black Uniform (Above)

Cap, Ring and Dagger of the SS
The dagger bears the inscription 'My honour is called loyalty', echoing the oath of the knights of Teutonic legend.

Communist Flag Burned in the Street

Boys of the Communist Youth in Berlin
Nazism's political adversaries, mainly Communist militants, were the target of large-scale, physical annihilation which aimed at rooting out any sign of dissent. (Below)

and the suppression of the SA put an end to the most openly aggressive faction of the party. At the same time, however, Hitler set up a bureaucracy of systematic repression against anyone deemed to be 'deviant' or an enemy of the 'community of people'. These changes were by no means kept secret; on the contrary, they were discussed openly in the newspapers, on the radio and every time Nazism was held up as a historic milestone.

The brutal repression against the left in 1933 was perceived by most Germans as assurance that from then on, any threat to law and order would be crushed, and by force if necessary. In the years that followed, the institutions set up to deal with the emergency were not repealed, but were actually strengthened in order to achieve a totalitarian control over society. Many private citizens reported neighbours, friends and colleagues, and even parents or children when they acted in a 'deviant' manner. These were spontaneous denunciations, not forced from on high, and their great number is clear proof of how the population used them to exercise some small form of social power or to get back at someone on a personal level. Thus, everyone became a potential enemy, a possible informer. It is precisely in this far-reaching erosion of the social fabric that one of the most significant consequences of the Nazi policy of terrorism can be seen.

The Internal Opposition

Society under the Third Reich was far more diversified and contradictory than its propaganda was willing to admit. There were many areas of open dissent, mainly the opposition organized by political parties. After 1932, the Communist Party was ready to go underground, and although it was the first

The SA Hauling an Opponent on to a Cart and Forcing him to Sweep the City Streets of Chemnitz in March 1933

victim of the terrorist violence of the new regime, it was not altogether unprepared for this new phase of the struggle; its militants carried out actions that were as dangerous as they were spectacular, causing many of them to be arrested, but failing to obtain concrete results. In 1935, in order to deal with the seriousness of the situation, this strategy of head-on clashes was abandoned in favour of less spectacular but more targeted initiatives aimed at organizing the potential for dissent that was spreading in the factories: party militants now had to be pervasive and certainly more fragmented, but less risky.

The Social Democrats were taken unawares by the changes introduced in January 1933, and for several months they thought they could find a *modus vivendi* with the new regime. When it became clear that no form of compromise was possible, the leaders went into exile – first to Prague and then to Paris – with the intention of organizing and directing the underground activities of the party members who had stayed in Germany. The majority of militant Social Democrats, however, abandoned political activity, though they remained faithful to their ideals at a personal level or within a narrow circle of contacts.

The ties between those who continued their activity underground and the leadership in exile grew weaker and weaker, and the link was soon no more than exchanges of information. The increasingly pervasive repression by the police put an end to all opposition on the part of working-class parties in 1938–39. In addition to the Communists and the Socialists, there were other small groups that were able to continue being active because of their greater organizational flexibility and due to the fact that they were less well known to the police.

Roll Call for Prisoners in the Oranienburg Concentration Camp on the Former Site of a Brewery.

HELMUTH JAMES GRAF VON MOLTKE IN 1928
One of the opponents of Nazism sentenced to death after the failed coup against Hitler in July 1944.

GERMAN JESUIT PRIESTS
The Jesuit order was placed under close surveillance by the regime. (Below left)

COMMUNIST MILITANTS PLAYING FOOTBALL IN FRONT OF PARTY HEADQUARTERS IN THE EARLY 1930S (Below right)

POPULAR DISCONTENT

Along with political opposition aimed deliberately at bringing down the dictatorship, there was a more covert and widespread discontent that displayed itself in actions and behaviour, manifestations of how people were getting frustrated with a regime that, in its goal of achieving total power over society, interfered in every single aspect of their daily lives. Examples of defiance against the Nazi regime included failure to enrol a son in the *Hitlerjugend*, not giving the 'Heil Hitler' salute, buying in Jewish-owned shops, and fraternizing with foreign workers; these were not acts signalling overall political repudiation, but specific misdemeanours. Many of these everyday actions were devoid of political overtones, and in a democratic society such non-conformist behaviour would have been tolerated. The regime, on the other hand, saw this kind of behaviour differently. Nazi totalitarianism politicized every sphere of society to the point of introducing political obligations even in the private sphere, thereby denying the right to any kind of political perspective. Rumours and complaints spread, especially concerning the poor quality or scarcity

Heinrich Mann (profile) and Albert Einstein

Jewish Child Refugees from Germany, Austria and Sudetenland Arriving in Britain in December 1938

German Jews Landing in Britain (Below)

of food and the slow pace of social reform. Hitler, however, was never the target of these criticisms, nor was he held responsible for whatever went wrong – it was a commonly held view that he was not even aware of problems. These undertones of discontent coexisted alongside a partial recognition of the regime, or at worst, a passive attitude towards the power of the state. It was just this sort of contradictory coexistence of different feelings that was one of the strong points of the Nazi system: in everyday conduct, the common person found it impossible to create a separation between feelings of dissention and passive acceptance or active consent.

Political Emigration

In 1933, many high-ranking officials, particularly of the working-class parties and trade unions, decided to leave Germany for security reasons. While the left-wing parties – Social Democrats, Communists and some smaller groups – created active and well-organized cells outside the Reich, there were far fewer members of the bourgeois parties who chose to emigrate, and on the whole they were more isolated. Between 30,000 and 40,000 people went into exile, settling mainly in France and Czechoslovakia, at least until the outbreak of the war. The choice to seek asylum in a country near Germany was based on the hope of a quick return, but also by the desire to maintain links with companions in Germany who were active underground. Thanks to the mediation of trusted contacts in the border areas, the Communists and Socialists managed to maintain a solid network inside the Reich until at least 1938. Their political activity, however, was almost exclusively limited to exchanging information; politically relevant news concerning the humour of the population was gathered and sent abroad, while newspapers and

THE BLUE ANGEL Maria Magdalena von Losch, stage-name Marlene Dietrich, became a cinema diva in 1930 after playing the part of Lola-Lola in the film *The Blue Angel.* Her rejection of Nazism took her to Hollywood and led her to apply for American citizenship. During the war, she sang for front-line American troops.

THE CONCENTRATION CAMPS

Just a few weeks after Hitler came to power, the whole German police apparatus was in the hands of trusted members of the SS, the SA and the Nazi Party. On 20 March, the first concentration camp was opened on the site of the former gunpowder factory in Dachau, near Munich. Other camps were opened after the arrests carried out by the SA and the SS. The following year, they began to be regulated: many of the improvized camps were shut down, and moves were made to clarify the situation of the prisons and of relations between the police and the SS. After the 'night of the long knives' (30 June 1934), which led to a showdown with the SA, the SS also replaced the SA in running the camps.

The years 1934–35 marked a change – fewer prisoners were detained, which led to some camps being shut down, and attempts were made to temper violence and abuse in the ramaining camps. Moreover, as Himmler shifted more and more police power to his own hands, Dachau became the model for other camps, particularly as regards the treatment of prisoners and internal rules. Here, indeed, due mainly to the efforts of Theodor Eicke who was then head of Dachau, the camp was organized in such a way that the tasks of policing were separated from those of surveillance. Between 1937 and 1938, as the regime strengthened its hold both in domestic and foreign politics, the new Nazi concentration camp system took shape, with four large camps – Dachau, Sachsenhausen, Buchenwald and Lichtenburg. Able-bodied men were the most frequently arrested, showing that the exploitation of manpower was becoming increasingly important. Many of the industries the prisoners worked for were under the power of the SS, so new camps were opened such as those in the vicinity of the granite quarries at Mauthausen and Flossenburg. The increasing numbers of inmates in these years was also due to an influx of prisoners from areas newly conquered by the Reich.

Jews were sent to the camps with the aim of encouraging them to emigrate; indeed, those who showed that they could were freed and allowed to leave Germany.

PRISONERS AT WORK IN A CONCENTRATION CAMP

NOSFERATU THE VAMPIRE (1922) BY FRIEDRICH MURNAU

books were sent into Germany. There was, though, no direct political influence from exiles. Even if those in exile claimed to be speaking for the majority of party members inside the Reich who were forced into silence, in reality the two were unconnected – those still in Germany were not in any serious way affected by the decisions taken by the emigrant groups. In point of fact, the political emigrés were plagued by the same contrasts and splits that had divided the working-class parties up to 1933. The only concrete attempt to create a common platform was made in Paris in 1936. Heinrich Mann, basing his efforts on the popular-front governments in Spain and France, tried to promote a *Volksfront* among the emigrés, but it never got beyond a common declaration of purpose, which the Socialists only adhered to as single individuals and not as a party. Political emigration did create a multitude of people denouncing Nazism and providing accurate analysis of the international situation, as well as many books, written principally by Communists. The outbreak of war triggered a new wave of exiles: the majority took refuge in England or left Europe for the United States or South America. Contacts within Germany were no longer possible, and groups who were still active turned their efforts, with limited success, to developing contacts with the Allies in an attempt to carve out a meaningful role in deciding military strategy and in formulating projects and plans for post-war Germany. After the war, the majority of emigrés returned to Germany and took up their political activism once again.

INTELLECTUAL EMIGRATION

The distinguishing feature of the exile from Germany was the high number of intellectuals who decided to leave: the most important writers (from Thomas Mann to Bertolt Brecht), directors, musicians, composers and actors left the country. For all of them, including the few who were already famous

ERNEST LUBITSCH IN HOLLYWOOD
After emigrating to the United States, the German director, pictured at centre below, directed Greta Garbo in the comedy *Ninotchka* (1939). In 1942, he shot the film *To be or Not to be!*, an ironic comedy set in Nazi-occupied Poland.

OTTO KLEMPERER AND THOMAS MANN
Both Klemperer and Mann chose exile in the United States; the former (profile) was conductor of the Los Angeles Philharmonic Orchestra from 1933 to 1947.

A SCENE FROM *METROPOLIS* (1926) AND THE EXPRESSIONIST-STYLE BILLBOARD FOR THE FILM DIRECTED BY FRITZ LANG
(Below)

abroad, it was extremely difficult to continue their activities. The first obstacle was language, and it was often impossible to finding an audience for their work. Many masterpieces of German literature were published abroad and some intellectuals, first and foremost Heinrich Mann, were untiring in promoting initiatives aimed at denouncing the regime. The line the exile press took came in particular from contributions by writers and journalists who had been active in the Weimar period. Amsterdam and Switzerland were the most important publishing centres, while up to 1939 the largest concentration of emigrants was found in Paris. It was here that many newspapers came out, representing the wide range of ideologies and cultural positions of the Weimar years; meetings, debates and initiatives of various sorts were held in the city, even though isolation was the most characteristic feature of life for the intellectuals in exile. For those who had moved to the United States, it was even harder to find work, although Hollywood offered new possibilities for some of the film directors, including Fritz Lang and Ernst Lubitsch.

The losses suffered by science in Nazi Germany were serious: roughly one third of professors and researchers were dismissed for political or racial reasons. Of these, two thirds left the country, creating significant gaps in fields that had enjoyed rapid development during the 1929s, from political studies to sociology, biochemistry to atomic physics. Often it was the younger scholars who emigrated, and who, mainly thanks to relief organizations, were able to find new positions, with the exception of physicians. The majority went to the United States without stopping in Europe, and their decision to abandon their native country was almost always permanent.

THE 'MYTH' OF THE FÜHRER

The myth surrounding the figure of Hitler grew throughout the 1920s alongside the evolution of the NSDAP through its various phases. The political and social crisis of the Weimar democracy led wide sectors of the conservative right to feel the need for a strong, authoritarian guide, a leader capable of guaranteeing national rebirth. In the Nazi Party's first year of life, Hitler saw himself as defender of the ideals of the movement and its chief spokesman, but not as the man called upon to change the destiny of the nation.
After Mussolini's March on Rome in October 1922, however, Hitler began to see his role differently. His followers began calling him 'the German Mussolini' and saw him as being capable of working miracles for the country as a whole. The turning point came with the Munich Putsch when, during the course of his trial, Hitler cleverly managed to overshadow the figure of General Ludendorff and came across as the only true leader of the extreme right. During his imprisonment, his followers cultivated the myth of the hero jailed for acting in the interests of the nation, and they became convinced of the need for the party's structure to be organized hierarchically. A clear sign of how the cult of the Führer had become a key element for the Nazi Party was the introduction of the 'Heil Hitler' salute in 1926.
In the years that followed, this image of a leader capable of overshadowing every conflict within the party became increasingly clothed in myth and at the same time became more convincing. During the years of the economic crisis, the idea of a strong power whose freedom of action would create the conditions for a crucial turning point gained increasing favour. After the Nazis' rise to power, it became clear to all those who had thought they could exploit the shock effect of the NSDAP only to dump the Nazis afterwards that Hitler was becoming more and more independent, and that the German people were giving him the exclusive credit for the regime's successes. After Hindenberg's death, the authority of the Führer knew no limits: the forms and structures of the regime depended solely on his will. The cabinet, which up to 1934 had met fairly regularly, met 12 times in 1935, but only on six occasions in 1937. Hans Heinrich Lammer, head of the chancellery, was the sole link between the Führer and his ministries. Although many decisions were taken directly by Hitler, he managed to stay aloof from day-to-day administration and any contrasts that arose, thereby confirming his intangible superiority. The outbreak of war brought swift military victories that made him even more popular. But when, from 1943 onwards, destruction by Allied bombing, hunger and cold began to dominate the daily life of Germans, the myth of Hitler began to crumble. It was the very charismatic nature of this myth and its messianic tones that made it impossible for it to turn into an alternative tool of power – its fall was inextricably bound to that of the Reich.

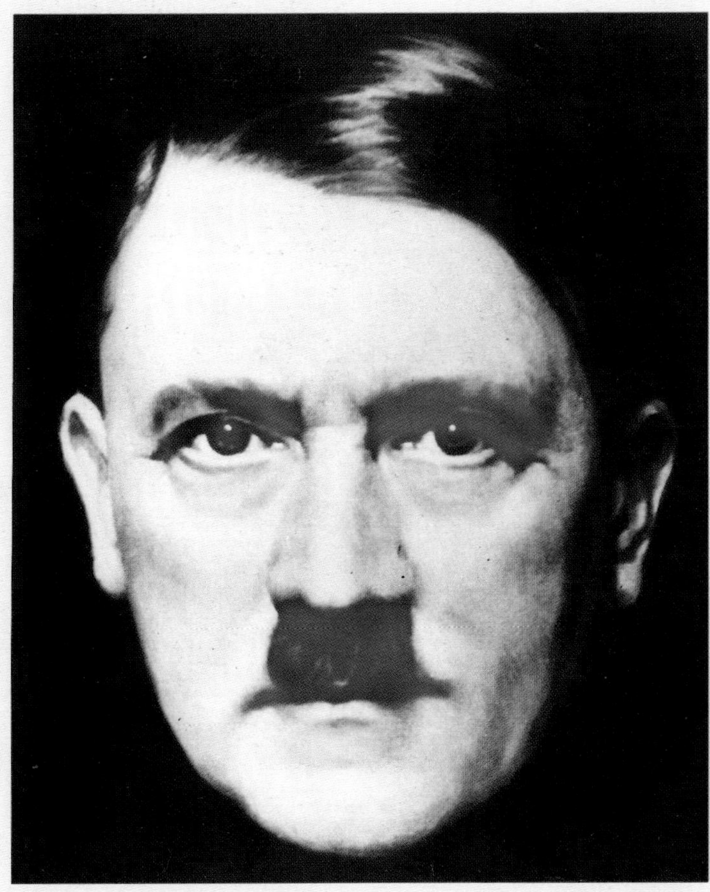

CLOSE-UP OF THE FÜHRER

PISTOL PRESENTED TO HITLER
It bears the inscription: 'To defeat the Red Front and the reactionary forces, and to protect our Führer.'

PORTRAIT OF HEINRICH KNIRR (1937)

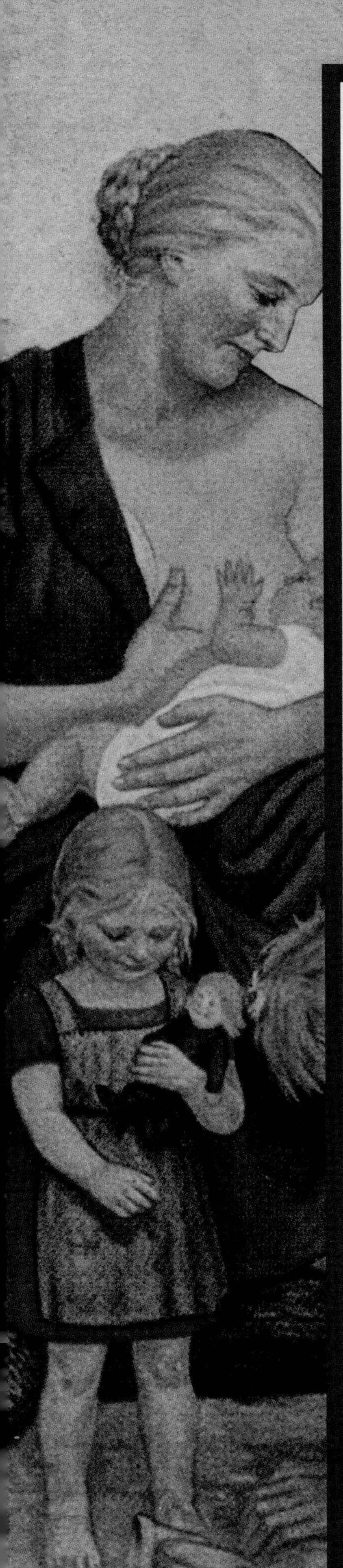

The Community

One of the foundations underpinning Nazi ideology was the clear distinction between everyone who belonged to the *Volksgemeinschaft* (community of people) and those who were excluded. The regime created an immense propaganda, ideological and repressive machine for indoctrinating and conventionalizing the community and discriminating against those who were not part of it. Immediately upon coming to power, the Nazis' main targets were their political adversaries, who were imprisoned in concentration camps for the purpose of 're-education'. Other minorities, such as homosexuals or persons held to be 'asocial', were considered undesirable and unworthy of belonging to the community of people, but they could, it was thought, be allowed back into society once they had changed their habits. By contrast, those who were considered to be racially inferior – specifically this meant the Jews, but also gypsies

YOUNG PEOPLE GIVING THE NAZI SALUTE
(page 96)

BUCOLIC DEPICTION OF THE FAMILY BY WOLFANG WILLRICH
(page 97)

ANTI-SEMITIC PROPAGANDA IN *DER STÜRMER* AND *SÜSS THE JEW*
The film *Süss the Jew* was made by order of Goebbels in 1940, with the precise aim of instilling Germans with hatred for the Jews.

Der Stürmer
Deutsches Wochenblatt zum Kampfe um die Wahrheit
Dank des Kronprinzen
Und der Sohn des Juden
Schächtmesser und Kreuz
Die Juden sind unser Unglück!

and the mentally ill – were forbidden to have any contact with Germans and were gradually but assiduously excluded from every part of society.

This ideological mystification that the regime set in motion was of primary importance; the appeal to the common sense of belonging was a driving force in strengthening collective discipline. The idea that every member of the community had a say, illusory or not, in his or her destiny, was a homogenizing factor for conduct that gave the impression of endorsing the regime's theory that it was a conflict-free society. In the wake of the legislative measures already in place, the exclusion mentality began to make itself felt in people's minds and they, too, began persecuting those officially discriminated against. The violence they used grew more extreme as the perpetrators became increasingly convinced of the ethical, as opposed to the political, reasoning behind their actions.

ANTI-SEMITISM

Anti-Semitism was common in most of Europe after World War I. Deep nationalistic feelings, but also more general conditioning and reasoning, lay behind its growth. First and foremost there was a feeling that civilization was drifting towards catastrophe, and that Europe and its hegemony was in decline; there was also the uneasy myth of a Bolshevik revolution powered by Jews. The stereotype of 'Judeo-bolshevism' became something of a buzzword and accelerated the speed of anti-Semitic feeling. One of the fundamental works of anti-Semitism, *The Protocols of the Elders of Zion*, described an alleged plot by Jews to take over the world, and it was distributed all over Europe in the inter-war years. The first German edition was published in 1919, and the book contributed to the spread of the idea that a conspiracy was taking place, behind which lurked powers of darkness that were invincible and therefore had to be fought against with

THE SA PLACARD PROCLAIMS: 'GERMANS, DEFEND YOURSELVES! DON'T BUY FROM JEWS!'

THE JEWISH ORGANIZATIONS

January 1933 was not seen as a turning point by most of Germany's Jewish population. On the contrary, many Jewish associations, especially the more conservative ones, hoped that they could be integrated into the new order. The other organizations followed their own political convictions and ideological leanings that had evolved over the years. German Jews had three options open to them at this point: total fragmentation in the face of Nazi terrorism; applying officialdom within their organization; or continuing the pluralist and democratic tradition that had characterized Jewish society since their emancipation. Most chose the last option, and it continued until the life of German Jews had been totally annihilated. The national organization that represented all groups in this period (*Reichsvertretung*) gained importance in these years. It never demanded official recognition from the government but it often appeared as the official organization representing German Jewry. Oddly enough, the Jews were the only group within the Reich to keep their self-governing structure based on democratic principles. Their commitment was focused mainly on assistance, education – including for adults – and culture. The growing influence of the *Reichsvertretung* within single organizations and in the life of every German Jew was one of the reasons why many Jews became aware of their Jewish identity during this period. The Nuremberg laws clarified their legal status but the *Reichsvertretung* duped itself into believing that it could continue its work with greater security than before. Furthermore, the hiatus called during the Berlin Olympics also led it to believe that the worst violence was over. Up until March 1938, the representative importance of Zionism grew, and to the young in particular it seemed a preferable alternative. Nazi political aggression increased and reached its peak in early 1938 with the *Anschluss*, which severely worsened the lot of the Jews: a law of March 1938 disbanded the communities. The *Reichsvertretung* was turned into a national association (*Reichsvereinigung*) with a more centralized structure than before, but it did continue its function of representation. It continued its intense cultural and spiritual activities in all the major communities for all these years, until the start of the deportations. Increased segregation into ghettoes did not completely break Jewish vitality, although it did condition it deeply.

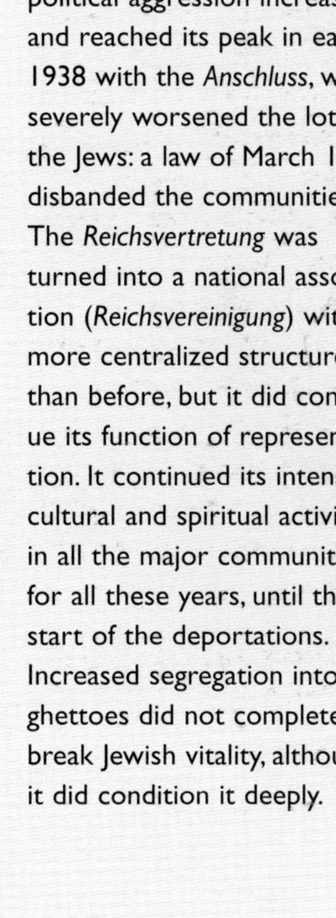

GERMAN CHILDREN IN A RABBINICAL SCHOOL
(Above)

***TALMUDISTS* (1934) BY MAX WEBER**

A Joyous Welcome for Julius Streicher
This illustration appeared in a widely distributed elementary school textbook; hundreds of thousands of copies were published by Streicher himself in 1936.

'Keep Clear of Jewish Doctors and Lawyers!'
An anti-Semitic poster in the street of a German city.

the greatest possible violence and effectiveness.

Nazism managed to take on board every aspect of anti-Semitic ideology that had emerged since the 1880s and, thanks to Goebbels and Julius Streicher, added virulence and a biological connotation. It was the prelude to a shift to extremism in the racial conflict. Jews, therefore, were not only considered racially inferior, but were also a permanent threat to the new order that was being worked towards, and were thus made the scapegoat for all the ills and hardships Germany was experiencing. Violence perpetrated against the Jews increasingly became a method of intimidation; racism, and anti-Semitism in particular, turned into yet another means for social control.

Racial Purging

After the March 1933 elections, violence against Jews continued to grow. On 1 April, the boycott against Jewish businesses that had been repeatedly called for by Nazi hardliners – old soldiers, SA members and rank-and-file party members – finally took place. The hardliners, however, never had enough power to force Hitler to take decisions against his will. The boycott received a cool reception by the majority of the German people, many of whom were in favour of limiting the presence of Jews but still wanted to buy in their shops. It was at this point that Hitler initiated a course of action that, in the years to follow, would be very typical of his anti-Jewish initiatives –

Father of All German Children
Hitler was unmarried and childless, and this was exploited by the regime's propaganda machine to strengthen the myth of his role as 'head of the family'. His charisma also came from his public appearances during which German observers saw him as possessing a magnetism that often led him to be compared with the Pied Piper.

COVER ILLUSTRATION FOR AN INFANT'S BOOK IN YIDDISH

seeming to compromise between the party hardliners and the more pragmatic line of the conservatives, and giving the impression to the public that the nuts-and-bolts details were being looked after by others. The first anti-Jewish law was passed on 7 April, and it dealt with the restoration of public-service career officials. Paragraph 3 – which was known as the 'Aryan paragraph' – stated that non-Aryan employees had to retire. Until then, the Nazis had harassed and boycotted Jews who were identified as such on mere supposition; there had been no formal denial of legal rights based on a discriminatory definition.

In the months that followed, the effect of the law was that Jews were expelled from all key sectors of the state; they were forbidden to work in the medical profession – so that the biological health of the national community would be safeguarded – and they could not practise law. They were even denied the chance to study – a law passed on 25 April that forbade the overcrowding of schools and universities laid down that new Jewish students in all schools could not exceed 1.5 per cent of the total number of students and in no instance could the number of Jews in a school exceed 5 per cent of the total number of students. On 14 July, a law revoking German nationality was passed, cancelling the naturalizations that had occurred between the end of World War I and 30 January 1933, and establishing a ban on the immigration of Eastern Jews.

HEREDITARY ILLNESSES AND STERILIZATION

In the 1930s, the regime passed a series of measures that excluded from the community of people anyone who could undermine its racial purity. A law passed on 14 July 1933 – the same day as Hitler passed another law, making opposition to the Nazi party illegal – enforced the sterilization of everyone with physical or mental defects: it was a turning point

JEWS IN A POLICE WAGON LOOK ON AS POLICE EXAMINE THEIR IDENTITY DOCUMENTS
Jewish citizens were deemed to be the greatest danger to Germany because they personified the threat of contamination of the Aryan race. In *Mein Kampf*, Hitler had written: 'Is their anything disgusting or any infamy, especially in the life of society, in which at least one Jew has not had a hand?'.

JEWISH EMIGRATION

Some 350,000 Jews fled from Germany during the Nazi regime. The period during which departures took place depended on what stage anti-Semitic policies had reached – the flow was constant over the years and reached its height in 1938 after the 'Night of the Broken Glass'. Finding a country to go to became increasingly difficult because the immigration policies of many nations set very low quotas; most of those who stayed in Europe went to Britain, while outside Europe the favoured destination was the United States. Even reaching Palestine was not easy because its leadership prohibited any large influx from Germany. Only a few of those who fled from Germany's racist regime began actively reporting what the Nazis were doing or in any way turned the spotlight on Germany. The main priority in what was predominantly an emigration of family units, as opposed to one of political or intellectual exile, was the reconstruction of the wherewithal to live. Most of the Jews who left Germany did so when they realized that the conditions for economic, social and physical survival no longer existed in that country. For many of them, the long, contradictory process of integration had begun in earlier decades, and accepting that this had now been lost was often a long, heart-wrenching process. Actually, very few returned to Germany after 1945: the Holocaust had caused too deep a wound.

Mural by Ben Shahn depicting Jewish immigrants in the United States led by Albert Einstein

'Jews Are Not Welcome'
The message on this caricature was placed at the entrance to a Prussian beer-hall.

in this process, and a keystone in legislation on eugenics and race. It introduced the principle of coercion in the sense that not only could family members apply for the handicapped to be sterilized, but so could doctors if they deemed it necessary. Wherever disagreement occurred, ruling was deferred to the *ad hoc* 'tribunals for hereditary health'. In addition to the operation that made men and women incapable of procreating, any care for the institutionalized was also withdrawn as an indirect measure to hasten their death.

Between 1933 and 1945, 400,000 people were forcibly sterilized, including alcoholics, the 'asocial', the handicapped and other groups seen as impure. In October 1935, one month after a law was passed banning Germans from marrying Jews, the 'law to protect the hereditary health of the German nation' was passed. This prohibited marriages between Germans and anyone who was undesirable to the community of people; it called for outside races, or groups deemed to be 'racially inferior', to be registered, and made it necessary for a marriage licence to state that the spouses were 'racially suited' for marriage. A supplementary decree forbade Germans to marry or have relationships with anyone of foreign blood in addition to the Jews; twelve days later, it was specified that the measure covered gypsies, blacks and 'their bastards'.

Just before war broke out in the summer of 1939, a systematic campaign to kill handicapped adults began, and it was presented to the public as a euthanasia project. It took place under a veil of secrecy – relatives were not told that their family members had been moved to murder centres that had been set up in various locations in Germany. Even before World War II initiated a new European order and the extermination of the Jews had begun, murder by the state had already been legally established and carried out on a large scale.

Regimentation of the Masses
The spread of anti-Semitism in Germany made use of pseudo-scientific theories based on racial concepts: the 'Aryan superiority' of the German people, whom the regime considered 'chosen' to carry out a civilizing mission to root out the 'Judeo-Bolshevik threat', had to be safeguarded at all costs.

ARYAN WEDDING
Germany experienced a rise in the number of marriages, which were also encouraged by material incentives provided by the regime.

CHILDREN BORN FROM 'RACIALLY PURE' MOTHERS AND THE MALE ÉLITE OF THE SS (Below)

THE GYPSIES

In 1933, gypsies represented 0.05 per cent of Germany's population. By and large they held regular jobs, even though these were often in itinerant trades such as horse-trading and within circuses. They had been subjected to police persecution before 1933 and initially, at least, the Nazis merely continued this policy but made it gradually harsher. Nazi propaganda demonized two areas of society: the foreigner, with his unacceptable culture, and the alleged asocial person unwilling to accept the discipline of a job and non-migratory, stable relationships.

This persecution was based on an alleged inferiority of biological heritage of a people considered to be deviants, and therefore, similarly to the Jews, gypsies were not deemed to be 're-educatable'. The only way to safeguard the purity of the community was to progressively bar gypsies from society; during the war, this meant they had to be exterminated.

From 1935, camps were set up to imprison gypsies. Conditions inside them were horrendous, they were surrounded by barbed wire and life in them was closely regimented. The largest camp was at Marzahn on the outskirts of Berlin, and it was camouflaged to hide it from the eyes of those participating in the Olympic Games. The discrimination took on a whole new dimension with the publication of the results of alleged research into the biology of the race in which a leading role was played by Dr Robert Ritter, Director of the Berlin Institute of Criminal Biology from 1936 onwards. In December 1938, Himmler gave orders for 'regulation of the question of the gypsies to be based on the nature of this race'. A decree dated 8 December, dealing with the 'struggle against the plague of the gypsies', made conditions under police detention even harsher.

THE *LEBENSBORN*

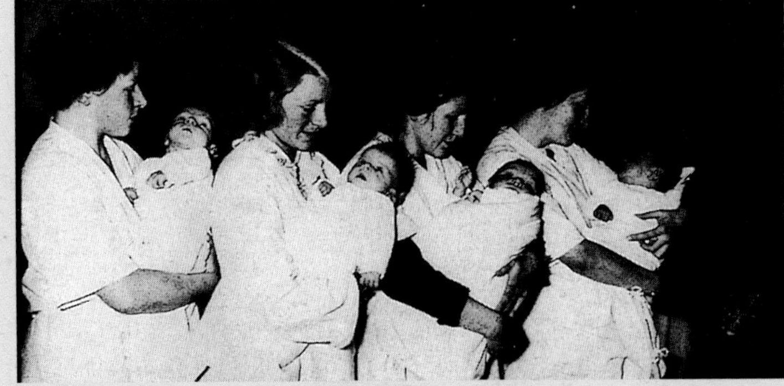

An SS association set up by Himmler in 1935, and funded by coerced donations from the SS, the aim of the *Lebensborn* ('Source of Life') was essentially to lend support to the regime's racist policies. *Lebensborn* members actively opposed abortion and supported an increase in the birth rate. Administratively, they were dependent on the economic division of the SS, but functionally they were linked to the SS department that dealt with racial issues. During the war, premises were opened to take in unmarried 'racially pure' mothers to mate with the regime's racial élite – namely the SS – and procreate 'healthy' children; eleven 'source of life' premises were opened in Germany and nine in the occupied territories of France, Belgium and Norway; it resulted in some 8,000 babies being born. Thus, in addition to implementing racist, anti-Semitic policies that aimed to expel all those 'unworthy' of living in Germany, the Nazi regime also actively promoted procreation even outside the family unit and the bonds of marriage that it was unflaggingly praising in its propaganda as the basis for a strong society. Faced with the need to safeguard the race, even the constituted order took second place.

Preis 30 Pfennig

Ritualmord-Nummer

Der Stürmer

alsches Wochenblatt zum Kampfe um die Wahrheit

HERAUSGEBER: JULIUS STREICHER

Nürnberg, im Mai 1934 | 1934

Jüdischer Mordplan

gegen die nichtjüdische Menschheit aufgedeckt

Das Mördervolk

Judenopfer

Die Juden sind unser Unglück!

DER *STÜRMER* ANNOUNCES THE 'JEWISH HOMICIDAL PLOT'
The magazine edited by Streicher unceasingly published illustrated articles about Jews raping Aryan women.

OFF ON THEIR HONEYMOON
Newlyweds on a motorbike festooned with the Nazi flag. (Below)

THE NUREMBERG LAWS

As the exclusion of Jews from German society intensified, the issue of physical or biological separation took on increasing importance. Mixed marriages and sexual relations between Germans and Jews increasingly became the target of violent attacks by the Nazi Party, with its press at the forefront; the *Der Stürmer* newspaper, edited by Julius Streicher, was especially hardline on the issue. In September 1935, the Nuremberg laws were announced during the 'Freedom Congress'. The 'Law on Citizenship of the Reich' stated that Jews, who were no longer viewed as equal citizens, were to be deprived of their political rights. The 'Law to Safeguard German Blood and Honour' banned marriages between Jews and Aryans. It also nullified marriages already contracted, prohibited extra-marital sexual relationships between the two groups, and made it illegal for Jews to have German women servants younger than 45 years old. In the months that followed, the issue of the so-called *Mischlinge* (people of mixed-blood) became prominent and it was ruled that whoever had three Jewish grandparents was *de facto* Jewish.

Subsequently, every area of daily life and every professional activity in which contact between Aryans and Jews could possibly have sexual implications, was identified and prohibited. Jews, for example, were expelled from public swimming pools; from spring 1936, most departments of medicine forbade Jewish students to conduct gynaecological examinations on Aryan women. Even after the Nuremberg laws were

THE POISONOUS MUSHROOM

Published in 1938, The Poisonous Mushroom *was one of the textbooks used in schools that showed most clearly how virulently anti-Semitism had spread throughout German society:*

Little Franz is out with his mother to gather mushrooms in the wood ... On the way his mother says:

'You see, Franz, just like mushrooms in the wood, the same thing happens to people on earth. There are good mushrooms and good people. There are poisonous mushrooms, mushrooms that are bad, and people who are bad. And you've got to look out for these people just like you do for poisonous mushrooms. You see?'

'Yes, mother, I understand,' replies Franz. 'If you trust bad people bad things can happen to you, just like if you eat a poisonous mushroom you can die!'

'And do you also know who these bad people are – these poisonous mushrooms – in humankind?' asks his mother. Franz looks very proud.

'Of course mother! I know. They are ... the Jews. Our teacher is often telling us that at school.'

'Right!' says his mother, pleased.

And then she turns serious and continues.

"Jews are bad people. They're like poisonous mushrooms. And just like it's hard to tell good mushrooms from poisonous ones, it's just as hard to see that Jews are villains and criminals. Just like bad mushrooms come in all sorts of colours, Jews, too, manage to camouflage themselves by taking on the strangest appearances."

'What kind of strange appearances are you thinking about?' asked little Franz.

His mother sees right away that her little boy has not yet understood. But she continues her explanation in an even tone. 'Well now, just take the wandering Jew roaming from town to town with his fabric and all kinds of merchandise. He boasts that his wares are the best and the cheapest but they're really the worst and the dearest. You're not to trust him. It's just the same with the Jew that deals in farm animals, the Jew in the marketplace, the butchers, the Jewish doctors, the Jews who have been baptized and so on. Even though they make us believe that they're nice and say a thousand times over that they only want what's best for us, we can't believe them. Jews they are and Jews they always will be. They are poison for our people ... Just like a single poisonous mushroom can kill a whole family, so a single Jew can annihilate a whole town, or city or even a whole people.' Franz now understands what his mother means.

'Mother, do non-Jews know that Jews are as dangerous as poisonous mushrooms?'

'Unfortunately not, my little one. There are many million non-Jews who still don't know what the Jew is. This is why we have to tell them, to put them on their guards against the Jew. We also have to put our youth on guard too. Our boys and girls have to be made to know what the Jews are. They have to know that the Jew is the most dangerous mushroom that there is. Just as mushrooms grow everywhere, so the Jew is found in every country in the world. Just as poisonous mushrooms often bring about terrible disasters, so the Jew is the root of poverty, pain, infection and death.'

CHILDREN READING *THE POISONOUS MUSHROOM* (Above)

ILLUSTRATIONS IN AN ANTI-SEMITIC BOOK
The first shows a Jewish teacher and children being expelled from school; the second shows Jews going into exile under a sign reading 'One-way street'.

Jewish Passengers on an American Ship Taking Them to Safety Across the Atlantic

Jewish Shopkeepers' Windows Smashed in a German City
From the 'Night of the Broken Glass' onwards, promoting anti-Semitism was the exclusive responsibility of the SS. (Below)

passed, most of the population was still against acts of violence against the Jews, but not against marginalizing them or depriving them of their civil rights. Since segregation was already enshrined in law, most people felt themselves freed of any responsibility for the measures that had been taken against the Jewish minority, whose destiny had now been shouldered by the state.

'Night of the Broken Glass'

The year 1936 marked the beginning of a new phase in anti-Jewish persecution. Full employment had been achieved and the anti-German front was showing signs of weakness; further measures against the Jews were therefore feasible. In this atmosphere of accelerated mobilization, the Jewish question took on a new dimension in the eyes of many Germans. With previously unheard-of virulence, the Jews were defined as a world threat, and anti-Jewish initiatives were exploited to justify the conflict about to break out. Hitler's speeches became ever more threatening and an accelerated process of Aryanization of Jewish assets began, partly as a result of the economic situation and partly down to the increased confidence in the business and industrial fraternities that there would not be any Jewish reprisals. In September 1936, the regime talked about Jewish emigration as a serious issue for the first time.

One of the big problems in rooting out Jews from German society was that they were an integral part of it at every level; the system had to continually come up with new ways of cutting these links. From early 1938, all Jews were made to hand in their passports, which were only returned to those wishing to emigrate. Everyone was registered and placed under surveillance – it was almost impossible to escape an increasingly widening net. A new series of laws passed in 1938 smashed what was left of the Jewish economy to smithereens,

RESERVATIONS: JEWS TRANSPORTED LIKE ANIMALS
Photo composition from 1939 by John Heartfield, a German Communist artist exiled in Britain. The image is dominated by Himmler brandishing a whip. Works by Heartfield are some of the most effective examples of art reflecting politics.

and in the summer of that year anti-Semitism re-exploded with extreme violence.

The date 9 November 1938 (known as the 'Night of the Broken Glass') was a watershed in the persecution of the Jews in Germany; state initiative moved on from discriminatory legislation to overt violence. The trigger for this was the assassination by a young Jew of Ernst von Rath, an official in the German Embassy in Paris. There had, however, already been a long-running press campaign to get the population primed for just such an event. The death of von Rath unleashed a violent reaction all over Germany: Jews were beaten up and ill-treated publicly, synagogues were set on fire and shops were pillaged. In the months that followed, new decrees enshrined Jewish exclusion from German society: by the time war broke out, their segregation into ghettoes was complete.

GERMANS AND RACISM

How much significance the majority of Germans gave to the 'Jewish question' is difficult to ascertain. Political stability, the dismemberment of the left, economic recovery, national reawakening and increasingly aggressive expansionist policies were all certainly more important in German minds than the vague outlines of anti-Semitic persecution. The concerns of everyday existence in a period of political change and economic uncertainty were what people focused most on, but the vast majority did not oppose the anti-Jewish initiatives. Identifying Hitler with a racist policy, and the knowledge that the Nazis were intent on pursuing it, may have increased

JEWISH WEDDING IN GERMANY

MOTHER AND SON Poster canvassing support for the women's association entrusted with raising the birth rate. During Nazism, German women did not merely think of themselves as 'custodians' of the home fires; they proposed a concept of motherhood that did not rule out getting involved in social matters and contributing to the country's economic growth.

ALFRED ROSENBERG

Rosenberg was born in 1893 into a family of shopkeepers, and in 1918 he graduated from Riga Polytechnic with an architecture degree. The territorial shifts that occurred after World War I meant that the city then became part of the Soviet Union, and in 1919, Rosenberg moved to Munich. Here he came into contact with the anti-Semitic extreme right and he threw himself wholeheartedly into political journalism. In 1920, he joined the German Workers' Party, which the following year became the NSDAP. He began writing for the *Volkischer Beobachter*, and became its editor-in-chief in 1923, a post he held (except for a break between 1924 and 1926) until 1937. He took part in the Munich Putsch, and during Hitler's imprisonment was active in organizing the party that replaced the disbanded NSDAP. In 1929, he established the Militant League for German Culture with the declared aim of freeing Germany from 'degenerate art'. He was elected to parliament in 1930 and dedicated himself to the country's foreign policy. In 1933, he became head of the party's office for links with Nazi organizations abroad, and in 1934 he was the 'Führer's appointee for overseeing the spiritual and ideological education of the NSDAP', a post that always set him at loggerheads with the Ministers of Education and of Propaganda. In 1939, he set up the Institute for the Study of the Jewish Question – essentially a body whose job it was to pillage libraries and art galleries, stealing all assets belonging to the Jews. When war broke out, he busied himself with purloining works of art from the occupied countries and getting them to Germany. In 1941, he was appointed Minister of the Eastern Occupied Territories. Rosenberg's greatest contribution to the Nazi Party was his capacity for developing various theories. His best-known work was *The Myth of the 20th Century* (1930); despite the book never being officially sanctioned by the Nazi Party, two million copies of it were printed. In it, Rosenberg advocated a new anti-Christian, anti-Semitic religion and, in the same vein as his other writings, he attempted to construct a new mythology of revolution that would eradicate all traces of the past and lead to the renaissance of a whole new civilization thanks to the strength of Nordic Aryan man. He was sentenced to death at the Nuremberg trials.

ALFRED ROSENBERG
Rosenberg saw history as being dominated by the fight between the values borne by 'Nordic' peoples and the lack of values of the racially impure.

A MEMBER OF THE 'ADOLF HITLER' DIVISION OF THE SS

ARYAN FARM WORKER AND CARICATURE OF A JEW IN A SCHOOL BOOK

***THE KALENBERG FAMILY OF FARM WORKERS* BY ADOLF WISSEL (1939)**
The figurative arts had the task of spreading the feeling of belonging to a 'community of people' based on Aryan supremacy. (Below)

the immobility, or perhaps even the passive complicity of the masses.

Although there was widespread acceptance of the segregationist policies and the expulsion of Jews from public and civil service, in general, little pleasure was taken in participating in the degradation. After the 'Night of Broken Glass', much criticism was voiced about the excessive violence used, and the waste and the damage to all these consumer goods, but very few people actively came to the aid of those being persecuted or raised their voice in protest against those responsible. There was an overriding passiveness and sense of acceptance which in itself provided implicit support for the more extreme forms of violence. But passiveness and acceptance feed on themselves, and the outbreak of war and the creation of the 'final solution' was to develop this attitude to its extreme consequences. This was one of the Nazi regime's greatest successes – where it failed to obtain open unconditional approval, it enjoyed at least passive silence.

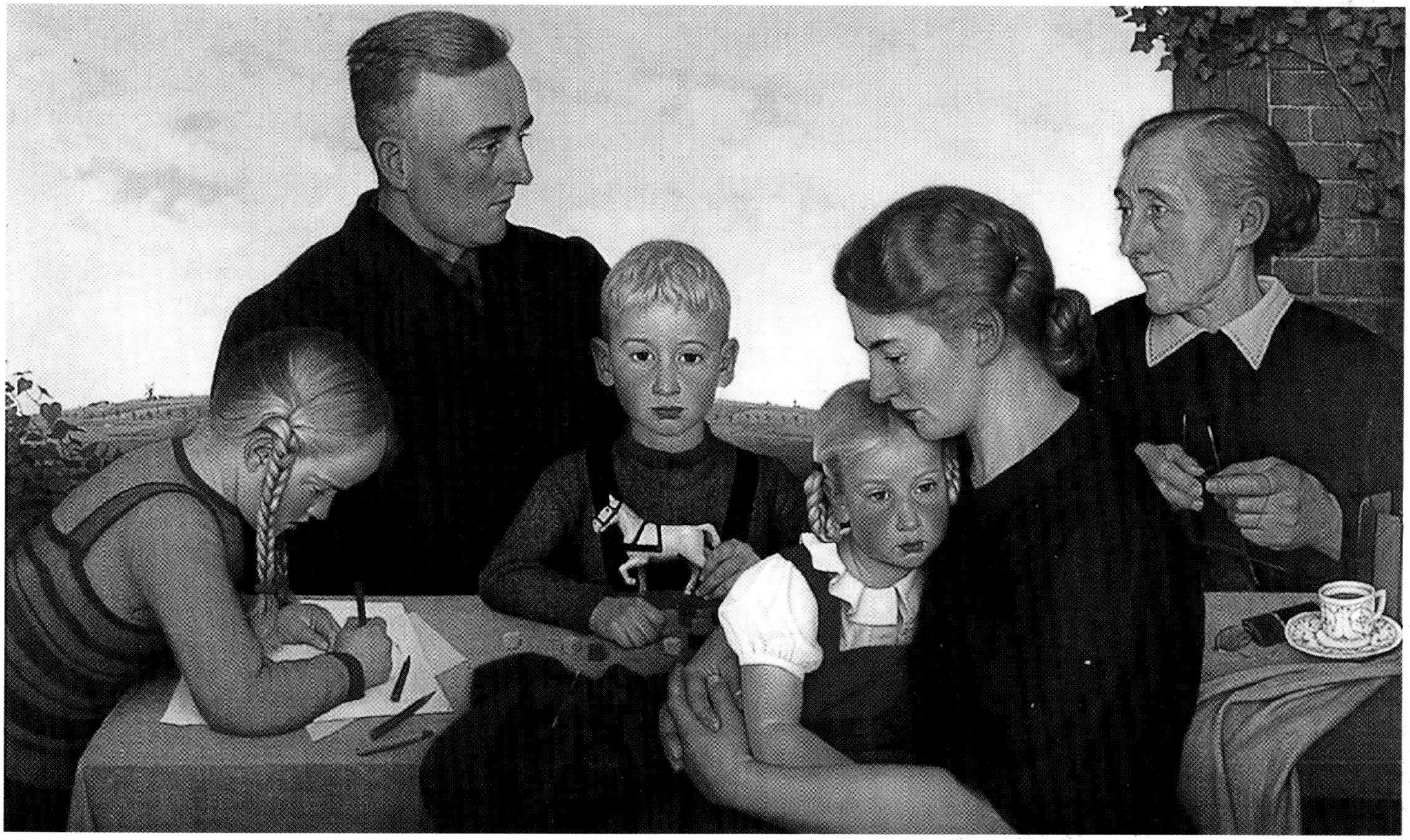

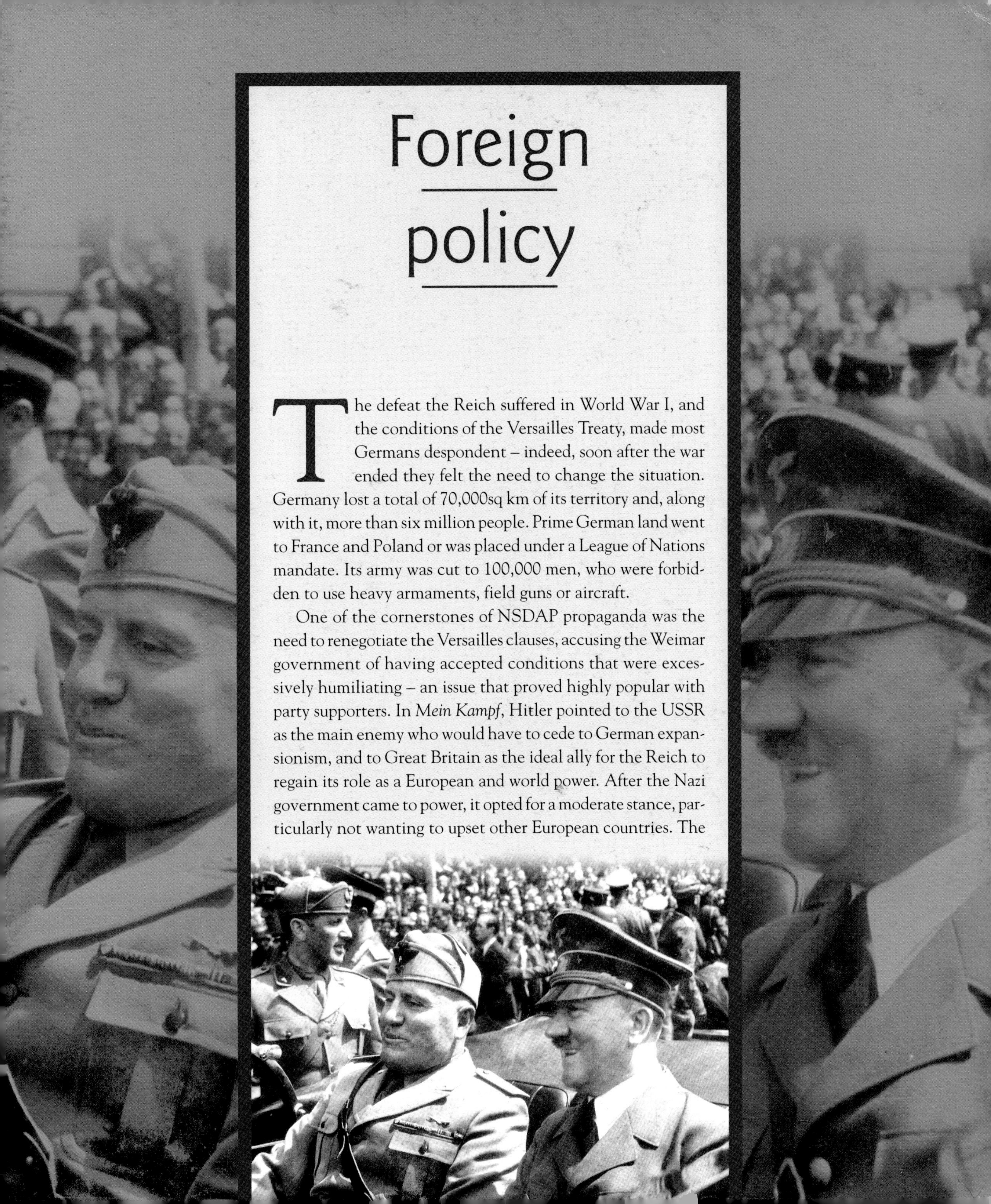

Foreign policy

The defeat the Reich suffered in World War I, and the conditions of the Versailles Treaty, made most Germans despondent – indeed, soon after the war ended they felt the need to change the situation. Germany lost a total of 70,000sq km of its territory and, along with it, more than six million people. Prime German land went to France and Poland or was placed under a League of Nations mandate. Its army was cut to 100,000 men, who were forbidden to use heavy armaments, field guns or aircraft.

One of the cornerstones of NSDAP propaganda was the need to renegotiate the Versailles clauses, accusing the Weimar government of having accepted conditions that were excessively humiliating – an issue that proved highly popular with party supporters. In *Mein Kampf*, Hitler pointed to the USSR as the main enemy who would have to cede to German expansionism, and to Great Britain as the ideal ally for the Reich to regain its role as a European and world power. After the Nazi government came to power, it opted for a moderate stance, particularly not wanting to upset other European countries. The

AN EAGLE GRASPING A CROWN OF OAK LEAVES WITH A SWASTIKA IN ITS CLAWS (Page 112)

MUSSOLINI AND HITLER (Page 113)

UNTER DER LINDEN
View by night of the scenery set up in Berlin's main avenue for Mussolini's visit in September 1937.

ZEPPELIN IN FLIGHT ABOVE NEW YORK (Below)

Treaty of Berlin, signed with the Soviet Union in 1926, was confirmed in May of that year. The concordat with the Vatican signed that same July was seen in a favourable light, especially by Catholic countries like Spain and Italy. Hitler's real aims, however, were all too clear. Germany left both the League of Nations and the disarmament conference, rejecting the strategy of collective security and claiming the right to make agreements without external restraints. Thus the way was prepared for the later phases of Nazi expansionism.

REVISING THE VERSAILLES TREATY

After abandoning the League of Nations, Germany launched a series of bilateral negotiations, primarily to avoid being isolated within Europe, but also to achieve improved conditions in wider international treaties. In January 1934, Germany signed a ten-year non-aggression pact with Poland with the sole purpose of assuring Polish neutrality should Hitler decide to attack Austria; the pact was never seen by Germany as placing any restriction on its expansionist policies.

After World War I, the Saar region came under League of Nations control, with the proviso that a referendum would be held in 1935 to decide whether to confirm the status quo, or whether it should be annexed to Germany or to France. The Nazi Reich deployed a vast propaganda machine to canvas for union with 'our German brethren', and on referendum day, 13 January 1935, terrorist and intimidatory tactics were widely used. Ninety per cent of the population of the Saar opted for annexation to the Reich, an overwhelming success for Germany which caused an immediate rise in its

GERMAN OCCUPATION OF THE RHINELAND

HITLER INSPECTING A DIVISION OF THE WEHRMACHT
(Below left)

BENITO MUSSOLINI
The bond between Italy and Germany strengthened when, during Italy's campaign in Ethiopia, Hitler offered Mussolini German coal to replace that from England. (Below right)

international standing – free elections had produced a clear majority in favour of the Nazi regime.

Two months later, Hitler reintroduced obligatory national service, breaching the terms of the Treaty of Versailles. In March 1936, German troops marched into the Rhineland areas that had been demilitarized since 1919, against the provisions of the 1925 Treaty of Locarno. Germany was setting out on a policy of aggression and the other European nations stood by and did nothing. The majority of Germans were wholeheartedly in support of this policy, which provided a new lease of life and restored dignity to their country.

APPROACHES TO ITALY AND INTERVENTION IN SPAIN

The Third Reich's relationship with Fascist Italy was marred by territorial disagreements, in particular regarding Austria. Here, Engelbert Dollfuss was in power – his clerical-Fascist government drew inspiration from Italy, but in May 1934, Dollfuss was assassinated by Austrian Nazis. While the circumstances surrounding his death and who was behind it are still unclear, it certainly provided yet further support for Hitler's plans for annexation. Differences between Hitler and Mussolini rose to the surface because Italy, fearing some kind of Nazi attack, lined up its troops on the Austrian border. The following year, however, the international situation began to change. Mussolini attacked Ethiopia to assure Italy 'a place in the sun'. The League of Nations deplored the act and decreed sanctions against Italy, though they were widely breached. Germany then offered economic aid to Italy, which drew the two

Women Making Bombs in a German Factory

Hitler and Franco
The Führer asked the *Caudillo* in vain to enter World War II alongside the Axis powers. (Below left)

Banner of German Communists Fighting in the Spanish Civil War
(Below right)

countries closer together, a situation that would gather momentum in Spain a year later.

In the summer of 1936, civil war broke out in Spain, and it soon escalated into an international conflict between Fascism and anti-Fascism. Germany decided to step in with a show of anti-Bolshevik strength and crush international anti-Fascist resistance at a time when France and Spain were governed by popular fronts made up of socialists and democrats with Communist support. Hitler seized the opportunity to put the new military might of the Wehrmacht to the test – with a massive deployment of men and arms, and using techniques of war that would later be put to use in World War II, he set up a territorial and logistical support base in the Mediterranean. The anti-Bolshevik alliance between Italy and Germany was defined during the Spanish Civil War that ended in March 1939 with the victory of the nationalists headed by General Francisco Franco.

Changes among the Military Top Brass

After the four-year plan came into force, the Rhineland had been remilitarized, closer ties had been forged with Fascist Italy and the country had participated in the Spanish Civil

German Submarine
Investing money in rearmament, which in 1936–37 accounted for over a third of the Third Reich's budget, brought full employment to the German working class.

Franz von Papen (left) and Marshal Wilhelm von Keitel
Wounded in World War I, Keitel was in the 'freikorps'. In 1938, Hitler appointed him head of the Reich armed forces high command. (Below)

War, the way was paved for another conflict. In June 1937, Werner von Blomberg, supreme commander of the Wehrmacht and Minister of Defence, passed a number of directives for the armed forces to set in motion 'joint preparation for a possible war' based on two hypotheses: a war on two fronts with its centre of gravity either in south-east Europe or in the west. Germany's sabre-rattling was loud and clear, and while a Franco-Russian front was deemed inevitable, the regime continued to hope for an alliance with Great Britain.

In a meeting with military chiefs that following November, Hitler set a precise timetable that coincided with how rearmament – provided for in the four-year plan – was to proceed. He also stated that his main objective was the destruction of Austrian and Czechoslovakian independence, after which he would move east. Blomberg and Werner Fritsch, supreme commander of the army, agreed in principle, but they expressed some technical doubts. The timetable for rearmament and the open crisis in international relations were such that Hitler now felt confident enough to place new personnel at the head of the military, a move that was officially justified by casting moral dispersions on the conduct of Blomberg and Fritsch. Blomberg was accused of marrying a woman of dubious morals and Fritsch of being homosexual. They were replaced in February 1938 by men totally dedicated to the Führer: Wilhelm Keitel was appointed supreme head

JOACHIM VON RIBBENTROP

Von Ribbentrop was born in 1893 and his father was a career soldier. He never finished his studies but moved to Canada with his brother in 1910 where he held various jobs. When war broke out, he came back to Germany and fought at the front where he was wounded in 1917. Since he had no professional training, he began work with a trader in Bremen when the war ended, and in 1919, he launched his own company for trading in wine; it was highly successful and by the mid-1920s he had made his fortune. Though he had no particular interest in politics, von Ribbentrop first made contact with the Nazi Party in 1930, joining it in 1932, and making very generous financial contributions to the party in those years. He made his villa in Dahlem – a residential area of Berlin – available to Hitler for the many political discussions held in the early months of 1933. That same year, von Ribbentrop was elected to the Reichstag and he began his career, firstly as the chargé d'affairs for disarmament in 1934 and from 1935 as ambassador to London. He was appointed Foreign Minister in 1938 to replace the overly moderate von Neurath. Von Ribbentrop's strong aversion to England and his preference for closer ties with Japan were quite distant from the position of Hitler. However, the Führer exploited von Ribbentrop's position to keep in favour with the conservative groupings aligned with the latter.

WITH THE JAPANESE FOREIGN MINISTER JOSUKE MATSUOKA AND DINO ALFIERI, THE ITALIAN AMBASSADOR TO BERLIN (1940)

VON RIBBENTROP IN 1938
Often accommodating to Hitler, in Göring von Ribbentrop had the toughest opponent to his anti-English foreign policy. He held some weight in planning the strategy of the Reich until halfway through the war, when his star began to wane. Captured by the English in 1945, at the Nuremberg Tribunals he was judged to have been one of the major protagonists responsible for World War II and sentenced to death.

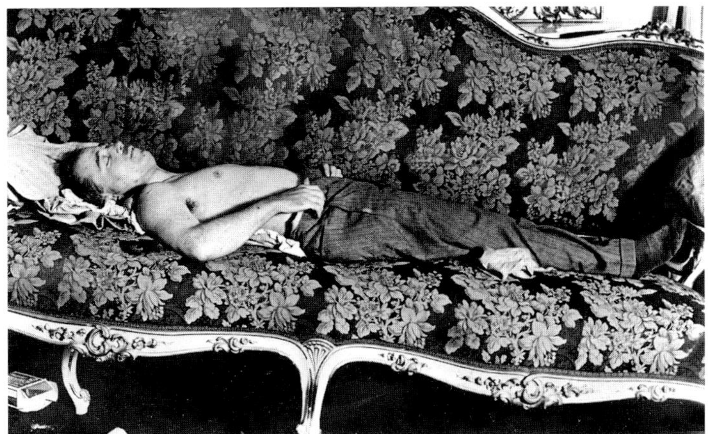

THE CORPSE OF DOLLFUSS
Architect of a corporative, authoritarian regime that outlawed all political parties, the Chancellor was assassinated in 1934 by the Austrian Nazis who favoured annexation to the Reich.

JOYOUS WELCOME
German troops marching into Austria in March 1938. (Below)

of the Wehrmacht and Hitler himself took on the role of Minister of War. At the same time, the Foreign Minister, Kostantin von Neurath, a conservative of the old school of diplomacy, was replaced by the dynamic, ruthless Joachim von Ribbentrop, testimony to how these changes were the prelude for an even more aggressive stance in Nazi policies.

THE ANSCHLUSS

In 1936, Hitler announced the four-year plan, thereby ensuring that everything would be in place when war broke out. By 1937, the international balance of power had shifted radically – France and Britain had shown themselves to be weak and generally uninterested in setting up any kind of opposition to Nazi expansionism, which was therefore able to carry on unhindered, and was aided by the forging of closer ties with Fascist Italy.

Austria was finding itself increasingly isolated on the international stage. On 12 February 1938, Hitler summoned the Austrian Chancellor, Kurt von Schuschnigg, and commanded him to entrust the Ministry of the Interior in his government to the Austrian Nazi Arthur Seyss-Inquart and to allow the Nazis complete *carte blanche*. On returning to Vienna, von Schuschnigg made a last-ditch attempt to salvage the independence of his country and declared a referendum on Austrian independence. This gave the Nazis an excuse to invade, and on the evening of 10 March, Hitler ordered his 8th army to march towards Vienna. The following day, Göring forced von Schuschnigg to resign and Seyss-Inquart proclaimed the annexation of Austria to the Reich. Thus the dream of a reunification of 'German brethren' and the creation of a 'greater Germany' was starting to become a reality.

Nazi Flag

The Antikomintern Pact
The foreign ministers of Italy (Galeazzo Ciano far left), Germany and Japan pictured at the signing ceremony of the 1937 alliance. (Below)

German troops marched into Vienna on 12 March to popular acclaim. The new regime unleashed a campaign of violent repression against political enemies and Jews and, in the space of a few short weeks, brought about a far-reaching purge that had taken several months when it had taken place in the Reich. On 10 April, a referendum confirmed the *Anschluss*, with 99.73 per cent voting in favour.

Berlin, Rome and Tokyo

Their cooperation in the Spanish theatre of war had made the alliance between Germany and Italy a solid one. At the end of October 1936, the Italian Foreign Minister, Galeazzo Ciano, went to Berlin and won recognition for Italy's empire in Ethiopia. Then during a speech in Milan in November, Mussolini proclaimed the birth of a Rome-Berlin axis. From then on, Italy provided systematic, albeit tacit, support of Germany's expansionism. For Hitler, the axis was mainly a means for trying to convince Great Britain to join the anti-Bolshevik alliance, while Mussolini was trying to broaden his sphere of influence to the detriment of Britain and France.

In the meantime, the Reich was trying to bolster its international standing, especially in the Mediterranean and North Africa, by making approaches to Japan. On 25 November 1936, the two countries signed the 'Antikomintern Pact' consisting of an agreement to cooperate in the repression of the activities of the Communist International as well as an additional agreement that bound the two not to strengthen the position of the Soviet Union should one of them be attacked. This treaty, openly aimed at combating Communism, was in reality a link for the aggressive warmongering policies of Germany and Japan, both interested in weakening the Soviet Union and in overturning the world order

THE PACT OF STEEL

On 22 May 1939, Italy and Germany signed the 'pact of steel' by which, with the thought of going to war, the Reich assured itself an alliance with the Fascist regime. Italy signed it without knowing what Germany had planned for Poland or precisely what the aims of the alliance were. Article 3 stated: 'In the eventuality that notwithstanding the wishes and hopes of the parties to this agreement one of them should find itself embroiled in belligerent complications with one or more of the Powers, the other party to this agreement will immediately ally itself to the former and will support it with all its military might on land, by sea and in the air.' This openly flew in the face of the general practice of international diplomacy whereby commitment to coming to the aid of another party was subordinated to it being attacked by third parties; in this case, attacking would trigger the mechanism of reciprocal assistance, so the pact favoured the imminent ambition of Germany to invade Poland. Mussolini himself understood the risks implicit in this clause as can be seen from a letter he sent Hitler a few days after stating that Italy would not be ready to enter war before 1943. Article 4 of the pact stipulated: 'In order to ensure the rapid application of the obligations provided for in the eventuality envisaged in Article 3, the two parties to this agreement will conduct a detailed analysis of their collaboration in military terms and in the area of war economics. Similarly, the two Governments will keep each other constantly informed of their respective adoption of measures necessary for the practical implementation of this Pact.' The term 'constantly informed' was immediately breached by Hitler – the day after signing the pact, he wrote a report to his military chiefs concerning preparations for war and said that an important premise for success was total silence towards Italy and Japan concerning Germany's operational objectives.

Hitler and Mussolini in the Piazza Della Signoria in Florence in 1938

German Soldiers in Prague
This photograph, taken in September 1938, clearly shows the anger of the Czechs about the decisions reached by the major powers in Munich. The conference paved the way for the expansion of the Reich towards central-eastern Europe, which had been left to its fate by French and British diplomats.

Hitler Entering Czechoslovakia
(Below)

without any form of international mediation. In 1937 Italy, too, signed the 'Antikomintern Pact', and two years later, in May 1939, just after the end of the Spanish Civil War and the dismemberment of Czechoslovakia, Italy and Germany signed the 'pact of steel' assuring each other mutual military support even in the eventuality that either unleash a war of aggression.

The Dismemberment of Czechoslovakia

The events in Austria made Hitler realize that he could act without France or Great Britain standing up against his strategy of eroding the shaky balance that was enshrined by the Versailles Treaty. Neville Chamberlain, the British Prime Minister, stated that he preferred negotiating with the German government as long as the Soviet Union was left out of every agreement; his choice of following a policy of appeasement contributed to speeding up the already rapid pace of Nazi expansionism.

A few days after the *Anschluss*, Hitler launched a violent and aggressive propaganda campaign against Czechoslovakia, where a German minority of some three million people lived. Berlin gave generous funding to Konrad Henlein, head of the Sudeten Germans, for him to press the Prague government for increasing self-determination. This included demanding the cessation of

GERMAN PAVILION AT THE UNIVERSAL FAIR IN PARIS IN 1937 The area allocated to the German pavilion was right in front of the Soviet Union's. Speer got to know in advance what the Russian pavilion was to look like, so he designed one for Germany that in size equalled if not surpassed that of the Reich's main ideological adversary.

THROTTLEHOLD
In this English cartoon Mussolini is shown being throttled by Hitler in an emblematic depiction of the role assigned to Italy by the German-Italian pact.

CONFERENCE OF MUNICH
From left to right: Neville Chamberlain, Edouard Daladier, Hitler, Mussolini and Ciano. (Below)

the Sudetenland (28,000sq km, or 20 per cent of Czechoslovak territory) to Germany on the assurance that, thereafter, Germany would make no further demands.

On 30 September, a meeting took place in Munich organized by Mussolini. The heads of the British, French and German governments signed the 'Munich Pact' that accepted the Nazi demands and sanctioned the annexation of the Sudetenland to the Reich. In so doing, France and Great Britain felt they had satisfied every claim the Nazis would make; but events soon proved otherwise. Hitler's intention was to expand the Third Reich eastwards: in March, Czechoslovakia was completely dismembered through the two-fold strategy of military pressure and stirring up internal unrest. Slovakia was forced to declare independence and claim protection from the Nazis. The Czech territories, with their high industrial potential and raw materials crucial for launching German expansionism, were placed under direct control of Berlin as the 'protectorate of Bohemia and Moravia'.

The path was now clear for attacking Poland.

THE NAZI-SOVIET PACT

In April 1939, Hitler decided that he would attack Poland before the year was out. The balance of international power was increasingly precarious, but neither France nor Great Britain made any stand against Germany apart from declaring themselves the guarantors of the Polish borders on 31 March. In April, Hitler revoked the 1934 pact of non-aggression with Poland and the naval pact with Britain of 1935. Even then, Great Britain and France did not form an alliance with the Soviet Union against Germany – mistrust and differences among them ran deep, and therefore negotiations proceeded sluggishly.

Nazi-Soviet Pact
German and Soviet officials draw the new Polish borders.

Peace Congress
A poster for the NSDAP congress that had to be cancelled because of the war.

Back From Munich
The British Prime Minister sought to halt the headlong rush to war, but his line of appeasement failed against Nazi-Fascist aggression. (Below)

Hitler was very skilful at exploiting the situation and played a cunning diplomatic game – he offered the Soviet Union normalized relationships and reciprocal recognition of each other's frontiers. On 23 August, a 'non-aggression pact' was signed between Nazi Germany and the Soviet Union which put an immediate end to years of violent propaganda and radical opposition to the Communist world. It stated that both parties would abstain from acts of reciprocal aggression; that should one of the two parties enter into war with a third party, the latter would receive no support from the non-belligerent signatory; and that peaceful means would be sought to solve every potential conflict. In doing so, Hitler thought he had forestalled a possible Anglo-French bloc that could emerge on his invasion of Poland; Stalin's idea was to keep his country out of any war that could break out among the capitalist countries, expand towards the Baltic countries and put a stop to Hitler's expansionist aspirations towards Soviet territory.

This pact threw the international Communist world into deep crisis because at a single stroke it nullified a ten-year struggle against the Fascist enemy. In fact, Hitler had not changed his plans at all and the pact safeguarded the Eastern Front for when he attacked Poland.

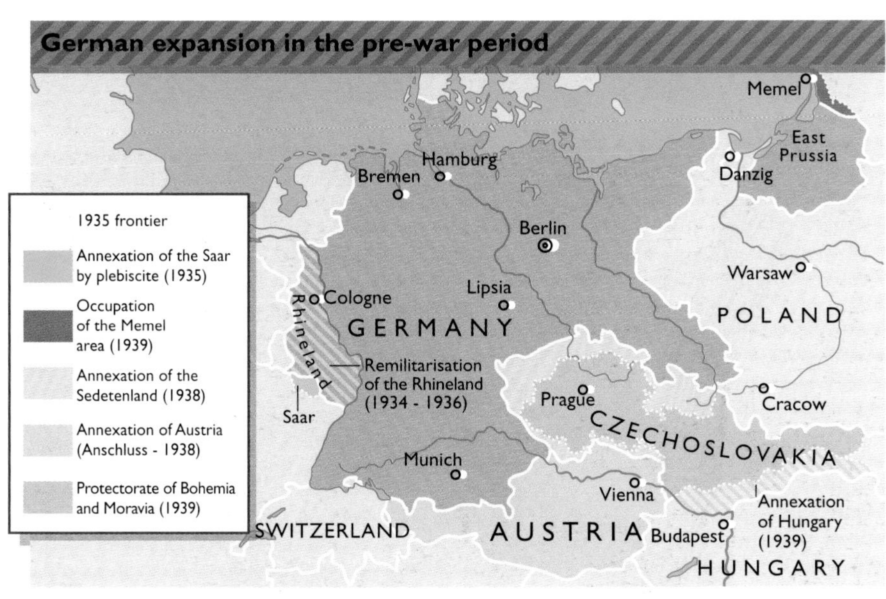

FASCISM IN EUROPE

There were many similarities between Fascist Italy and Nazi Germany: the creation of a power that tended towards totalitarianism, suppression of any kind of pluralism, the role of the dictator, regimentation of the masses and a corporative economic and social structure. The term Fascism can serve to define these regimes, which also held great sway at international level with their ideal model for solving the problems of a Europe beset to a lesser or greater extent by economic crisis, unemployment, nationalist resurgence and anti-Semitism. The regimes established under Nazi occupation during World War II were not imposed from the outside but came about as a result of the aspirations of the nations concerned which, although perhaps not necessarily predestined to evolve into fully-blown Fascism, did have many features in common with it. The 1930s thus witnessed a shift towards Fascism in many countries whose institutions and constitution were becoming increasingly

VNA GRANDE LIBRE

PLVS VLTRA

Ejercito Español

En atención a los méritos contraidos en Operaciones de Guerra por Brigada Helmut Karstedt

S. E. el Jefe del Estado y Generalisimo de los Ejercitos Nacionales ha tenido á bien concederle la Cruz de Guerra

Y para que conste y para satisfación del interesado, expido en nombre de S. E. el presente diploma en Burgos a 30 de Septiembre de 1938, III Año Triunfal.

El Ministro de Defensa Nacional

Ministerio de Defensa Nacional

anti-democratic and authoritarian, or were military dictatorships. What differed was that in these countries there was little of the grass-roots consensus – in particular on the myth of the leader and the organization of the young – that characterized Fascism in Italy and Germany. Austria was a clear example of autonomous development towards authoritarianism. The main characteristic of this regime and its strong church-Fascist leanings was the alliance between the governing Christian-social party and the *Heimwehren*, the Fascist-supporting militia funded by Mussolini. The most significant stages in its development were the brutal repression of the workers' movement

(February 1934) and the coming into force of a new anti-democratic, corporative constitution (May 1934).
In Spain, the Falangists played a central role from about 1933 in uniting the moderate and reactionary right around a religion of patriotism. Unlike the other dictatorships, the Spanish regime took shape during its civil war, which served to shift the internal equilibrium among the reactionary forces. For the whole period of Spanish Fascism, therefore, the ideological weight of the Catholic Church and the military might of the armed forces grew alongside each other. In Portugal, the strongly organic concept of the state was expressed in its new constitution of 1930, and in particular in the introduction of a corporative structure in 1933. Hungary and Rumania also saw the autonomous development of strong Fascist movements: the former's Party of National Will (established in 1935) and the latter's Iron Guard (which had already won 16 per cent of votes in the 1937 election) shared especially virulent anti-Semitic beliefs.

Certificate From Franco's Government to German Soldiers Who Fought in Spain (Above left)

Parade in Traditional Costume in Central Europe (Below left)

Rumanian Marshal Ion Antonescu With Hitler (Right)

2491

The war

One of the characteristics of World War II was the complexity of factors that led up to it. But it is easy to see how the aggressive nature of the Nazi Reich was the root cause of its outbreak. The war was first and foremost a clash for supremacy between powers, but also between ideologies and regimes – between Fascism and anti-Fascism – despite the enormous differences that separated the Western democracies from the Soviet Union. The anti-Fascist aspect of the war was especially visible in Europe where Nazi-Fascist aggressiveness was felt most directly, while the war between the United States and Japan was mainly a result of both nations trying to expand their respective spheres of political and economic influence.

Stuka Squadron in Flight (page 128)

The Swastika at the Arctic Polar Circle (page 129)

A Unit of Polish Lancers

Hitler with the German High Command Before the attack on Poland (Below)

World War II was far more a 'total war' than the Great War, both in terms of the increased involvement of every resource of individual nations and also in how opposing plans for a total restructuring of European society were felt as never before; not only over vast physical areas, but also in legal and social systems.

German warmongering took the form of a full-blown drive for the extermination of many parts of Europe. This was immediately evident in the attack on Poland and was behind the thinking for aggression against the Soviet Union. Indeed, the plan was not merely to defeat the enemy, as in the west, but to annihilate it in order to obtain territory for the Reich. In turn, the war of extermination generated phenomena typical of this type of conflict – resistance and underground movements evolved in the countries occupied by the tripartite axis in which collaborationist regimes and alliances were countered by movements of resistance against the occupying forces.

The war aims of the major powers were determined first of all by the need to stem the expansionism of Nazi Germany. This was carried out at different stages by Britain, the United States, the Soviet Union and the minor powers, even though each country had some axe of its own to grind: Great Britain wanted to defend its supremacy in the Mediterranean and the Indian subcontinent, and the United States was evolving from being a military arsenal to a world superpower. The balance between defensive warfare and the conquest of new space was particularly evident in the Soviet Union. Italy, in its role as a German ally, was to all intents a satellite of Germany, hoping to create a sphere of autonomy for itself. However, its status was more smothered than strengthened by this policy.

Drole de Guerre
A cartoon from April 1940, showing Hitler hooked by a French fish; it alludes to the hiatus in military operations prior to the attack on France.

Warsaw Street After German bombardment
(Below)

The Attack on Poland

At dawn on 1 September 1939, and without declaring war, Germany invaded Poland. For some months previously, the Nazi regime had decided on the use of force. The pact of steel with Italy, growing contrasts with France and Britain and the Nazi-Soviet agreement were all contributing factors to the growing international isolation of Poland. The war was waged according to the principles of *Blitzkrieg* ('lightning war'), with many armoured vehicles deployed in a multi-pronged attack on its centre. On 3 September, France and Great Britain declared war on Germany. The Polish army was in trouble from the start and it soon became clear what the outcome would be. Warsaw, almost completely destroyed by German bombardment, surrendered at the end of September and the armistice was signed a few days later. The western territories were annexed to the Reich, the central part formed the 'General governorate' under Hans Frank and the eastern lands were occupied by the Soviet Union in accordance with the Nazi-Soviet pact. During the Polish campaign, the Nazi regime put into practice the type of warfare it would use over the following months: surprise and brutality of attack to rapidly crush the enemy's armed forces, terror to paralyze the civilian population and 'fifth columns' to destroy their adversary from the inside. While the situation on the Western Front was stationary, the conflict spread in other directions: on 30 November, the Soviet Union attacked Finland, speeding up the German plan to conquer the Scandinavian peninsula for its iron ore deposits. On 9 April, Germany invaded Denmark and Norway; while the former was rapidly overcome, the latter, thanks to support from the British navy and air force, held out until 10 June. The Reich, intending to cut Great Britain off, launched an offensive on the Western Front.

French Prisoners
The attack on France was a masterpiece of military planning on the part of the German high command. Repeated encircling manoeuvres by the Reich's armoured divisions managed in just a few months to annihilate an army and a defence strategy thought to be invincible. (Below)

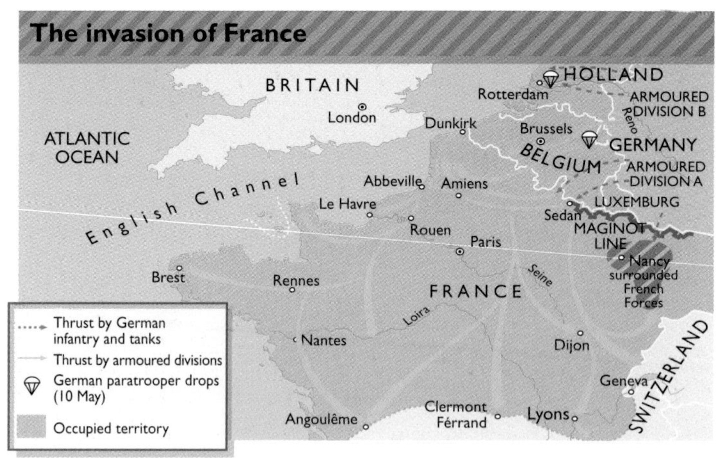

The Attack on France

On 10 May 1940, Germany moved into Holland, Belgium and Luxembourg – again without declaring war – and defeated them quickly through massive aerial bombardment. On 24 May, German troops drove on to the English Channel at Dunkirk where they called a halt. This allowed the British forces and the many French divisions to be evacuated, possibly with the German hope that this would induce Britain to cease hostilities. The Nazi troops advanced as far as the Meuse and the Ardennes, breaking through the French rear line between the Somme and Aisne; on 14 June, they marched into Paris, and the armistice was signed on 22 June.

The fall of France was the high point of Nazi triumph in the west, highlighting the weaknesses in French military strategy. The internal resistance, split politically and bereft of morale, also succumbed. The country was partly occupied; the German zone stretched to north-central France and to a strip along the Atlantic coast down to the Spanish border that included most of the industrial areas and all the Atlantic ports. Most of south-central France came under the control of the new Conservative government led by Marshal Pétain in Vichy. Hitler believed that a French government should continue to exist on French soil in order to stop it moving to Britain, where it could have continued to fight with much greater freedom. He did not demand the fleet be placed under his command nor did he advance claims on France's colonial dominions. His principal aim at that moment was to weaken Great Britain and stop it from uniting with what was left of the French forces. Hitler's aim was to pump France's economic resources dry in the service of Germany and to install a French government that would keep up the semblance of national sovereignty.

THE WEAPONS OF THE REICH

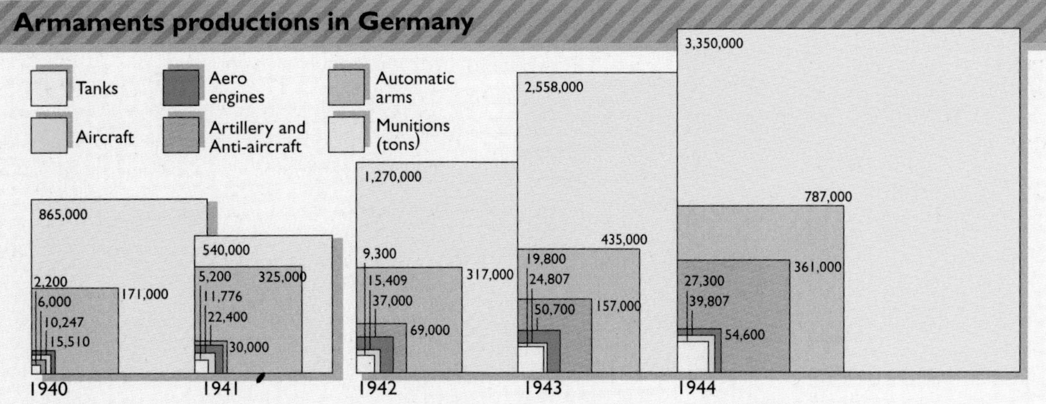

When Germany went to war, it could count on a well-stocked arsenal designed for a *Blitzkrieg*. After mandatory conscription was reinstated in 1935, the Wehrmacht became stronger, and in 1939 it had almost three million men and more than 3,000 tanks. The navy had been deliberately penalized; after the 1935 naval treaty with Britain, which allowed the Reich a fleet comprising 35 per cent of its British counterpart, Admiral Erich Raeder assembled an ambitious plan of naval reconstruction, but by 1939 it had only reached the initial stages. Internal disagreements had set the navy at loggerheads with the air force and Hitler stepped in to swing the balance in favour of the latter through the figure of Marshal Göring; the air force, both ground- and sea-based, was henceforth to be under the command of the Luftwaffe. Admiral Raeder was unable to put sea warfare under a single chief, a joint commander of the sea and air forces, and in 1939 it only had a couple of squadrons for coastal surveillance. The German navy ran the risk of not having support from the Luftwaffe when it was most needed because Göring was sure he could achieve supremacy at sea by using the air force alone. Indeed, the Luftwaffe had reaped the benefits of unlimited funding from 1933 onwards and had given itself an organization and a reserve of means devised and put together according to the most up-to-date technology. However, the factories had been built and equipped hastily, and mass production only began in 1938. Despite this, though, by 1939 the Luftwaffe had more than 4,000 planes. During the conflict, and especially from 1943 onwards when the prospects of victory were looking increasingly bleak, propaganda talked of Germany's possession of secret weapons. German scientific research had come up with new discoveries that would have revolutionized the war at sea and in the air but, with no benefits to ground-based forces, they contributed nothing to improving the Eastern Front. Significant developments were made, particularly in submarines and jet-powered aircraft, but the weapons that Hitler thought he could deploy to reverse the outcome of the war – even as late as 1944 – were the pilot-less V1 and V2 rockets launched specifically against London, but which brought about no change. Despite still having the strength to cause the deaths of hundreds of civilians, the Reich had by this point lost the war.

Base For Launching V2 missiles
The Vergeltunsgswaffen ('Arms of reprisal') were developed towards the end of the war. The V2 was a 12,900kg rocket equipped with about a ton of explosive, and had a flying speed of 5,600km/h.

SAFEGUARDING THE VITTORIA DI SAMOTRACIA IN A PHOTOGRAPH FROM SEPTEMBER 1940
After the German attack on Paris, many works housed in the Louvre were moved to safe keeping to prevent them from being damaged by bombing. The looting of paintings and sculptures in Nazi-occupied Europe by the Reich army was one of the most disgusting aspects of Nazi domination.

GREEK PARTISANS
Greek resistance was a thorn in the side of the Axis occupation troops.

THE 'DESERT FOX'
Erwin Rommel, seen pointing, was the most brilliant strategist of the war. As he was close to the protagonists who organized the attempt on Hitler's life on 20 July 1944, he was arrested and then forced to commit suicide. (Below)

The defeat of France was the first real political and military triumph of Nazism – it meant the defeat of a historical adversary and it marked the eradication of every enemy force from continental Europe. Operation 'Sea lion' – the attack on Great Britain – was, however, postponed, and the Reich was forced to move into Greece and Yugoslavia alongside Italy in order to avoid the latter's defeat in April 1941.

THE WAR IN NORTH AFRICA

In January 1941, Hitler decided to assist Italian troops who were getting bogged down in Libya. Two armoured divisions were sent under the command of Erwin Rommel, and they were known as the 'Afrikakorps'. Tireless and lightning-swift in decision making, Rommel very soon won himself the nickname 'Desert Fox', and as soon as he arrived he launched a lightning war on his own initiative. Helped by the vacuum created by British troops moving over to Greece, Rommel started to push forward, taking no heed of the opinion of the Italian high command to which he was supposedly answering. In April, he re-conquered the area of Cyrenaica, almost reaching the border with Egypt where he was involved in a long battle for the supremacy of Tobruk. He managed to conquer it in June the following year, taking full advantage, as he often managed to do, of a series of mishaps suffered by the British troops in the Mediterranean.

The 'Afrikakorps' continued their advance, and by the end of August were about 100km from Alexandria. The situation was becoming increasingly desperate for the British because their supply line depended on controlling the Suez Canal and holding the airbases in east-central Egypt. On 23 October 1942, General Bernard Montgomery, who had received crucial reinforcements, launched a counter-

HEINZ GUDERIAN
Guderian was the greatest theoretician of the war. He won resounding successes in the invasion of the Soviet Union and brought his Panzer division to the gates of Moscow.

A DESTROYED GERMAN ARMOURED VEHICLE
In November 1941, it was clear that the *Blitzkrieg* that was to have led to the defeat of the Soviet Union had failed. (Below)

offensive against the Axis forces, concentrating at El Alamein. The Italian-German forces suffered a crushing defeat and had to retreat into Libya. On 8 November 1942, after careful preparation made possible by the increased involvement of the massive American war machine, Anglo-American forces landed in Morocco and Algeria, and on 13 November, the British re-conquered Tobruk. In January 1943, Rommel abandoned Libya, and in May of that year the Anglo-Americans forced the Italian-German troops to surrender in Tunisia.

OPERATION BARBAROSSA

On 22 June 1941, the Nazis launched an attack against the Soviet Union. It was composed of 153 divisions, and Italy assisted with an ill-equipped, ill-prepared expeditionary force; Rumania also sent the majority of its army. Hitler intended to win the campaign in just a few months and at the beginning everything went more or less according to plan. Just as in the Polish and French campaigns, the Germans initially gained supremacy in the air and then unleashed joint manoeuvres using overpowering forces. They then homed in on the adversaries' Achilles' heel, supported by armoured vehicles and the air-force.

The early attacks overpowered the Soviets. In September, Leningrad was besieged, and by October the German forces were at the gates of Moscow, where they stopped. Autumn had arrived, and although the Red Army had suffered crippling losses it had not been wiped out. In December, in the middle of a Russian winter for which the Nazi troops were unequipped, the Red Army launched a counter-offensive. The 1941 Russian campaign marked the end of Germany's

RED ARMY PARADE
The lightning-fast German push into Russian territory was made easier by the surprise factor and by Moscow's lack of military preparation.

GERMAN MACHINE-GUNNERS IN THE SNOW
The German army found itself fighting in terrible conditions during the long Russian winter. (Below)

illustrious phase of *Blitzkrieg*; this tactic cost Germany a few losses, but they were more than compensated for by the wealth of plunder, the territory won and the enemy population conquered. However, the hardships experienced at the front line and defeats during the Soviet counter-offensive generated deep dismay among the German generals and the troops became extremely demoralized. It was necessary to replace the dead and injured and replenish armaments; the conflict deteriorated into a war of attrition that had the potential to drag on indefinitely with neither side poised to win. Germany was obliged to mobilize its every resource and every last man in an attempt to win, even though this meant taking manpower away from factories and key posts within the Reich. All of conquered Europe now had to be exploited so that the 1,000-year Reich could make its dream of glory come true.

THE NEW EUROPEAN ORDER

From the aggression against the Soviet Union onwards, Germany's warfare underwent a radical change: the National Socialist idea of war – not just conflict between powers but a head-on clash between ideologies and races – was given free rein. The aim was to conquer unlimited amounts of living space, guaranteeing the Reich immense resources and the creation of a 'new European order', namely a system of satellite states under Germany's thumb. This objective involved occupation which had to be perceived as definitive, as Nazi domination was planned to be. Indeed, it was in the areas earmarked for German settlement where this process of 'Germanization', so inseparably linked to racist ideals, took place. It involved settlement by Germans – the bearers of superior racial values – and the expulsion of huge numbers of the local population, leaving their work and their belongings to the

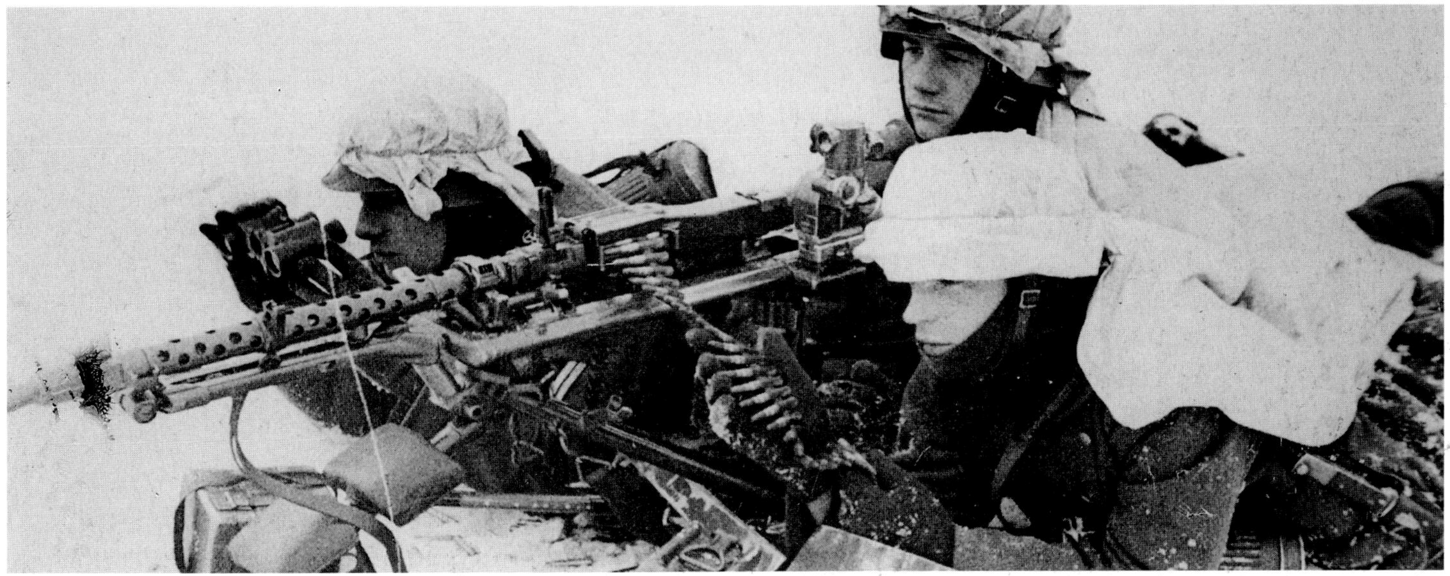

THE BARBARIZATION OF THE CONFLICT

The occupied zones were administered in accordance with the dictates of Nazi ideology rather than the rules governing rights of peoples. In the east, German soldiers were fighting an ideological war of extermination following rules that, with few exceptions, were shared by the whole Wehrmacht. On 22 August 1939, a few days before invading Poland and speaking to the military chiefs of staff, Hitler declared: 'In the first place there is the annihilation of Poland. The objective is to eliminate its vital forces, not to advance to a given point. Even though war may break out in the west, Polish annihilation is still our top priority. In view of the time of year, a rapid decision is called for. I shall provide the propaganda reason for launching the war – credible or not it doesn't matter. The winner is never asked afterwards if he was telling the truth. In launching and waging the war what matters is not the right but the victory. Close your hearts to mercy. Proceed in a brutal fashion. It is necessary to give eight million men justice – it is necessary to assure their existence. The strongest will be right. Be as harsh as you can.' On 6 June 1941, shortly before attacking the USSR, an order from the Wehrmacht supreme command was issued on how to treat political commissars: 'The troop must be aware of the following:

1. In this struggle an attitude of indulgence and respect of international law concerning these subjects is misplaced. They are a danger for its security and a swift pacification of conquered territories.
2. Political commissars are promoters of barbarous, Asiatic methods of combat. It is, therefore, necessary that they be proceeded against immediately and with the greatest possible harshness. This means putting them to death immediately upon capture in combat or in acts of resistance.'

French Partisans Before Being Shot (Above) **and Russian Prisoners** (Left)

Operation Barbarossa

1941 borders
Borders of the Reich
Main German thrust
Surrounded Russian pockets
Front line – 1 September 1941
Front line – 5 December 1941

Refugee Children
In addition to destroying many cities, the war caused the forced exile of millions of people.

German Propaganda in the Occupied Countries
A poster in Flemish encourages enrolment in the SS. (Below left)

Infantry Soldiers on a Tank on the Don Front
(Below right)

newcomers. In the economics of Nazi warfare, these massive population shifts became a tool for decimation and for selecting ethnic and social groups through the total collapse of states and of social fabric; redrawing the borders and devising a hierarchy of nationalities was all part of this single plan to transform Europe. It meant principally exploiting manpower in the most varied ways: putting it to work in production near where the manpower resided, using it in the service of the German war effort, or deporting it to be utilized in factories, agriculture and in the Reich's concentration camps. Another aspect of this process of 'Germanization' was the exploitation of factories and natural resources in a massive one-way process of continental integration – a system of total subordination of the requirements of the periphery to those of the German Reich.

The Internal Front

The war also changed everyday life for Germans. Food rations got smaller and smaller, the quality of the bread got worse and the absence of nutritious food became chronic. The working week rose from 48 to 50 hours. The longer the war stretched out, the more conscription looked towards German youth. Boys aged between 14 and 18 were forced to take part in courses run by the *Hitlerjugend*

'Men of the North – Fight for Norway Dutchmen: the SS Calls You!'
Propaganda in occupied countries.

Goebbels in a Russian Caricature
The Minister of Propaganda seeks in vain to transform the Stalingrad rout into the heroic resistance of the 1,000-year Reich against the "Bolshevik hordes". (Below left)

Russian Infantry on the Attack
(Below right)

that were ever more slanted towards war. They also had to replace the men in agriculture and in administration who had been drafted to the front. Propaganda became feverish and the war became a growing part of life in the classroom: soldiers on leave came on organized visits to schools to give enthusiastic talks on their experiences, classroom walls were festooned with maps charting the glorious advance of the Reich, and the number of propaganda leaflets produced grew exponentially between 1940 and 1941.

Instruments of internal repression were made harsher, and the terrorist apparatus of the regime was brought into action to intimidate and discipline every layer of society way beyond the mere hierarchy implicit in the ideals of *Volksgemeinschaft*. As the military suffered setbacks, the regime increased the pressure. To counter the loss of confidence that was spreading rapidly among the population after the defeat at Stalingrad, Goebbels made a notable speech at the Berlin indoor sports stadium on 18 February 1943. In it he used rhetoric to arouse the fanaticism and will to resist of the German nation, leading up to the question, 'Do you want total war?'. The threat of terror was also heightened, and in August 1944, under Operation 'Storm', some 5,000 ex-officials and politicians of the Weimar Republic were rounded up and sent to concentration camps. The last remaining prerogatives that the Wehrmacht had in matters of internal policies were done away with and the 'German People's Militia' was set up, compulsory for every male between 16 and 60. But when the first bombs started to fall on German cities, the civilian population began to get first-hand experience of the horror of war, and it became increasingly difficult to underpin credibility to the myth of the superiority and invincibility of the Führer and the Third Reich.

PROFESSOR ILCHENKO OF THE MOSCOW CONSERVATOIRE PLAYS THE VIOLIN FOR RUSSIAN TROOPS POSTED TO THE SOUTHERN FRONT In a photograph by one of the most famous Soviet war reporters, an infantry division listens to music after a day of fighting. © Anatoly Garanin/Magnum Photos

STALINGRAD

Hitler attacked the Soviet Union hoping to defeat it in a few months. After the first overwhelming successes, the advance ground to a halt when the harsh Soviet winter found the German army unprepared. At the gates of Stalingrad, one of the most decisive clashes between the two blocs took place for over a year. The initial resistance and the later offensive of the Red Army from 1942 onwards was seen by the whole world as a symbol of fighting back against Nazi aggression and represented the most solid hope for the Allied powers to be able to overturn the conflict. For the Nazi Reich, the Battle of Stalingrad was a huge loss in terms of men and machinery. Almost a quarter of the Axis forces engaged in the Russian campaign, mostly German soldiers, perished in the siege of the city. Goebbels immediately understood that it was necessary to cover up the event and make it look like a victory; during the struggle to defeat Bolshevism, Stalingrad became the symbol of the heroic German resistance against the barbaric advance of the Soviets.
The regime's propaganda machine declared the beginning of 'all-out war'; every means of state repression was tightened and every person called upon to do his or her part in saving the Fatherland.
The 'myth' of the Führer, however, began to crumble, and the internal front began to fall apart. It was the first step towards an increasing rejection of the war and the tragic consequences it entailed.

Russian Infantrymen Fighting Among the Ruins of Stalingrad
Winning back the city on the Volga destroyed the myth of invincibility of the Wehrmacht. (Above)

Tanks Blocked by the Cold and Machine-gunners in a Trench (Left)

MONUMENT TO SOVIET PIONEERS IN A STALINGRAD SQUARE The massacre that took place during the days when the Third Reich was celebrating its tenth anniversary shook the faith that Germans had in the Nazi regime. At the same time, the epic victory of the Red Army reinforced Stalin's position as the undisputed political and military leader of the Soviet Union.

Ration Queues in France
Until November 1942, France – three-fifths occupied – was officially free in the south-central area led by a collaborationist government in Vichy.

German Officers in a Paris Cabaret (Below)

The System of Nazi Power in the War Years

The bureaucratic and administrative apparatus of the Third Reich fell progressively into chaos. The last cabinet meeting had been held in February 1938, and during the war ministers and political chiefs found it progressively more difficult to gain direct access to Hitler. Power was being increasingly concentrated in the hands of just three men: Hans Heinrich Lammer, head of the Reich chancellery; the ever-present and hyperactive Martin Bormann, Hitler's private secretary; and Wilhelm Keitel, commander-in-chief of the Wehrmacht between 1938 and 1945. Every directive, measure or message from the Führer was exclusively drafted and made known by one of these three men.

Hitler was cutting himself off from the outside, and Bormann made sure that the Führer had as few contacts as possible with ministers, Gauleiters and party heads, even when they were former soldiers. From the outbreak of the war, Hitler spent more and more time in his headquarters, from where he also directed military operations. In January 1945, he moved to his bunker under the Reich Chancellery in Berlin, and he didn't leave it until his death.

After the failure of the air attack on Britain in 1940, Göring's power fell into decline. It was Goebbels, Himmler and Speer – all loyal to the chief to the very end and in continual rivalry among themselves – who jockeyed for power. Each within his own sphere of activity, they continued with the insane course of the Nazi-instigated war.

FOREIGN LABOUR

During World War II, almost eight million foreign civilians and prisoners of war were deported to Germany to be exploited by German industry, especially in arms production and agriculture. All in all, foreign workers constituted almost one-third of the labour force for the war effort, and in some instances – such as in the Krupp tank factories in Essen – it reached 50 per cent. They came to the Reich from all the countries that comprised the 'new European order' project. Recruitment began in Poland in 1939, but it was not as successful as had been hoped, so the Nazis began forcing the issue by rounding up everyone who was fit for work. Up to 1944, more than one and a half million Poles were deported to Germany. 1942 saw the beginning of a mass transfer of civilians (some two and a half million) from the Soviet Union because the prisoners of war working in the country were subjected to extremely brutal treatment and were unable to perform the heavy tasks they were forced to undertake. In March 1942, Hitler appointed Fritz Sauckel, Gauleiter of Thuringia, the plenipotentiary for labour recruitment; Sauckel then launched a massive rounding-up campaign in Nazi-occupied Europe and established a rigid racial hierarchy regarding how the victims were treated. At the top were workers of German extraction, while Soviets and Poles were confined to the lowest rungs. Living conditions and pay varied depending on what the job was. This hierarchy was also maintained and made harsher by the regime to stress the differences between the foreign workers, making it difficult for them to make alliances and fraternize.

FRITZ SAUCKEL
Saukel was behind the forced labour system that employed millions of Russian prisoners of war. (Left)

FRENCH WOMEN WORKING IN A GERMAN FACTORY

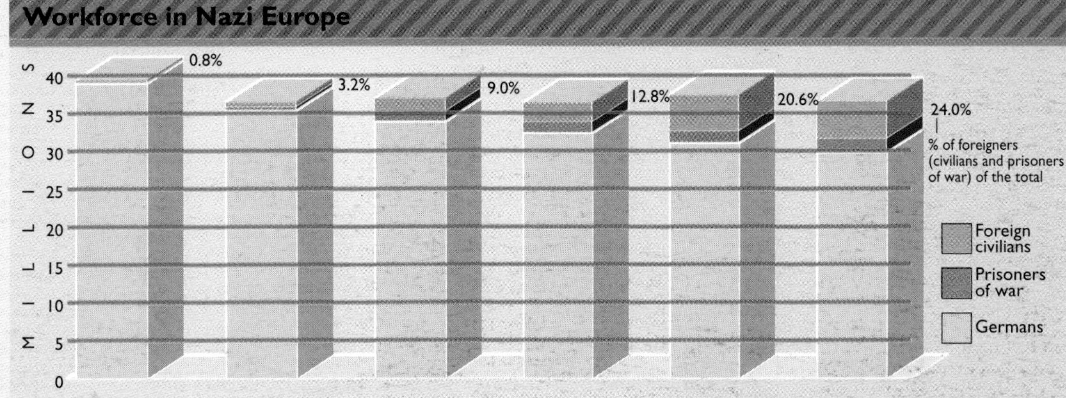

THE OCCUPATION OF ITALY

On 5 September 1943, Italy signed the armistice, putting an end to three years of a disastrous war. The crown was saved, but the whole country remained in the hands of the German army which, soon after Mussolini fell on 25 July, had begun calling in reinforcements. Germany's main aim was to put the Italian production potential – its agriculture, industry and labour force – to full use. A rounding-up process began, indiscriminate and often unplanned, with the aim of deporting as many Italians as possible to the industries of the Reich. In subsequent months, the recruitment was organized through bodies that were set up for the purpose, including the Todt organization. The Nazi occupation was characteristically brutal in the extreme despite there being a substantial difference between its war-like conduct in other places such as eastern Europe, and its attitude to Italy or France, where the Nazis did not carry out a systematic plan of demographic and territorial reconstruction. Whatever the country, aggression and arbitrariness were considered legitimate. The oppressiveness of the regime was not seen merely in how it reacted to rebellion on the part of the population, and massacres and reprisals were not always in a cause-and-effect relationship in with what had occurred, but further shows of strength. Violence as a demonstration of military superiority was an everyday occurrence. In addition to capturing and deporting unarmed Italian soldiers, there were measures for punishing the civilian population as a whole. Intimidation was a basic ingredient in the acts perpetrated by the German army; shows of strength against partisan Italian fighters were increasingly aimed at the civilian population, and rounding up became one of the main tools by which the Nazis displayed their domination of the territory. Almost 7,000 Italian Jews were deported to Nazi extermination camps and the police force in the Republic of Salò helped to capture them and organized the convoys that took them to their deaths.

American Soldiers Entering Naples in September 1943

Allied Cargo Ship Hit by a German Bomb off the coast of Sicily

THE WEST WALL
Behind the fortifications in reinforced concrete, German command had lined up its armoured divisions to repel the expected Allied attack.

MESSERSCHMIDT ME-262
The first jet aircraft, produced by German industry in 1942, the Me-262 was only used in combat from July 1944. (Below)

ECONOMICS AND ARMAMENTS

A law of 4 September 1939 stipulated a 50 per cent rise in income tax and higher taxes on the consumption of a whole range of products. This, however, was insufficient to cover arms expenditure, and the rest of the money came from contributions wrung from the occupied countries. Although it was placing the Reich under considerable fiscal strain, the Nazi regime tried to stem rising prices in order to keep discontent under control. In the end, it resorted to printing paper money and running up a massive state debt, but despite the inflation of payment instruments, the regime was able to maintain monetary stability for four years. Up to 1943, at least, the standard of living of Germans was higher than it was in Britain.

Despite entering the war with a relatively modern arms industry with double the output of Great Britain's, Germany was really only equipped for a short-term conflict. The organization of production for the war effort was placed with Göring, the man responsible for the four-year plan, which made him senior to the Ministries of the Economy, Labour and Supply. Fritz Todt controlled the Armaments Ministry as well as the national labour enterprise that bore his name, and both were virtually independent. In February 1942, Speer took the place of Todt (who had perished in an air crash) and from then on, absolute priority was given to the armaments industries. Speer broadened the committees inaugurated by Todt to include specialists from industry, not from the military, and who were asked to devise the best way of manufacturing each weapon. Although Speer was theoretically under Göring, and only responsible for armaments for the army (and not for the navy or the air force), in reality he took overall command of the war economy. Production

COLLABORATIONISM

Collaborationism occurred in many countries caught up in World War II. The regimes that the Nazis set up in occupied countries went well beyond what the needs of war called for, affecting the political and institutional organization of the country. Within the framework of the 'new European order', resorting to collaborationism was to have been a means for aggregating consensus around the idea of expansion of Nazi Germany. The collaboration of elements that were already part of the social and administrative fabric of the occupied territories was of primary importance for the Wehrmacht; not only in propaganda terms to assert the function of the Third Reich in its crusade towards a new Europe, but also in the more practical aspect of marshalling forces to serve Nazi Germany. Collaboration, however, was a one-way street. The Reich needed it in the occupying countries to save men and means; to get itself into the administrative apparatus and into the social circles that it could not do without; to round up supplies and transport industrial and agricultural produce from the occupied countries to Germany; to recruit the workforce it needed for its war effort; and to pass reassurance down through the known faces of local intermediaries. Many pro-Fascist and pro-Nazi movements offered to cooperate with the occupying power – a fundamental aspect of collaborationism – hoping that this would give them the chance to bring their political aspirations to reality. Often, however, and paradoxically in appearance only, Nazi Germany preferred to rely on the established power structures – as in Belgium, for example – rather than on Fascist forces, but structures that had a strong nationalist strain. The Italian Social Republic was a good example of how the Germans often considered local forces more of a hindrance than a help in the implemention of their policies.

French Woman With Shorn Hair
Punished for having had a child with a German soldier.
© Robert Capa/Magnum Photos (Above)

Jacques Doriot
The collaborationist leader of France (in dark uniform) fought as a volunteer in Russia.

Poster of the Belgian SS

'You Are at the front'/ 'You're Working and We're Fighting, Both For Victory!'
German workers are encouraged to make every effort to win the war.

German Battleship in Combat (Below left)

Wehrmacht Soldiers Buying Postcards (Below right)

for the war effort continued to rise, although it never reached the level of the American arsenal.

The Financial System of the Greater Reich

German military expenditure rose from 41 billion marks in 1939 to 60 billion in 1940 and 91 billion in 1942. In order to meet this, the Minister of Finances, Walter Funk, fell back on taxation and a system that has been defined as 'tacit funding': private individuals were encouraged to save and the banks were obliged to turn the funds over to the state in exchange for treasury bonds. For such massive expenditure, however, a much more refined and complex system was called for, and on 10 August 1942, Göring spelled it out to the Reich commissars and military commanders: 'I shall pillage beautifully and organize real hunting parties.' In every country they entered as victors, German military units sacked, pillaged and stole. Later, though, the occupying authorities abstained from such brutal measures, and opted for more underhand but equally effective alternatives. One of the first was an arbitrary revaluation of the mark – which by then was a pan-European currency – over the currency of the vanquished nation. This limited individuals' power to purchase German products by making them dearer, but enhanced the purchasing power of Germans in occupied countries. The first to benefit from this were the soldiers.

THE BOMBING OF DRESDEN

During the Casablanca Conference, Churchill convinced Roosevelt that in order to hasten Germany's defeat and maximize American firepower in Europe, aerial bombardment would have to be stepped up. The aim was three-fold: to destroy the Reich's military, industrial and economic power; undermine German morale; and pave the way for the landings in France by weakening the enemy's defence capability. An American airborne squadron was based in the south of England. While the English continued their night raids on large towns, the Americans flew by day to hit military targets. The peak of the carpet bombing was reached on 13 February 1945, with a raid over Dresden that lasted 14 hours and cost 135,000 lives. Viktor Klemperer, a Jewish philologist and former professor at Dresden University, had been keeping a diary for years; it was one of the most interesting documents of what everyday life was like under Nazism. When the bombing took place, he had not yet been deported because having married an Aryan woman, he had been spared the 'final solution' that had been the fate of most of the victims of the Polish extermination camps. What saved him was the destruction of the city. The pages of his diary dealing with the bombing of Dresden are a testimony of this tragic event:

'That was when we heard the main warning signal. – "If only they would smash everything!" remarked Frau Stühler bitterly. She had been very busy during the day in an attempt, apparently vain, to get her boy back. If things had stopped after that first attack I would always have remembered it as the most frightening one up to then, whereas now the later catastrophe coming on top of it just becomes a part of the general scheme of things. Very soon we began to hear the droning of the squadrons as they got closer, increasingly threatening and ever more deafening, the light went out and an explosion was heard nearby. ....A break, and we managed to get our breath back; we were kneeling bent double among the chairs, some groups were groaning and weeping; they got close again, the grip of mortal danger again, and more explosions. I lost count of how often all this happened. All of a sudden, the cellar window in front of the back entrance way got blown out and outside it was as bright as day. ... Then everything calmed down and the all-clear sounded. I had lost my sense of time. Outside it was as bright as day. In Pirnaischer Platz, Marschallestrasse, on the banks of the Elbe and on the other side, the city was in flames. ....There was a great open space in front of me, with nothing there, unrecognizable with a great big crater in the middle. Crashes, flare-ups bright as day, explosions. I wasn't thinking about anything, I wasn't even afraid; all I could feel was a frightening tension, I think I was expecting the end to come .... I had lost my sense of time, it was an eternity, and then in the end, it didn't even last long because then dawn started breaking. The city was still burning'.

Bomb Damage in Cologne
In this photograph taken from a British reconnaissance aircraft, the cathedral, the Hohenzollern bridge and the railway station are all visible. (Above)

Dresden
A view of the city in 1946.

Wehrmacht Soldiers Standing in Front of the Temple of Delphi in Central Greece

Frontier Crossing-point Between Occupied France and the Republic of Vichy (Below)

Economic relationships were thus begun that seemed perfectly normal. Commercial transactions shifted enormous quantities of merchandise to Germany. The trade of occupied Europe was directed towards the Reich and its satellites. In central Europe, the domination that Germany had achieved before the war became a monopoly. The plan of a 'new European order' provided, for instance, that after the war Germany would keep a sort of monopoly of European industry to itself, especially in metalworking and chemistry. Berlin was to become the centre for the arts, literature, fashion and the performing arts.

The costs of maintaining the occupying armies were covered by the occupied countries; the amount was not calculated on the number of soldiers present but on the supposed wealth of each nation. The substantial amounts of money were used by the Reich to pay the foreign labour employed in Germany in their own currency, and to buy its way into the national economic systems of other countries. Germany, which began the war with no foreign exchange reserves to pay for its purchases, postponed the payment of its growing debts until after the end of the war. To cap the inflation that inevitably ensued from this policy, the Reich took control over the national banks of every occupied country.

ROBERT CAPA
'The greatest war photographer', pictured here before the Normandy landings, worked in Spain during the civil war and then in China. His pictures documented the conflict in the East and in Europe. In 1946, together with Henri Cartier-Bresson and David Seymour, he set up the Magnum photographic agency. He died in Indochina in 1954. © Robert Capa/Magnum Photos

AMERICAN SOLDIERS WITH A NAZI FLAG (Below)

THE SECOND FRONT AND THE CHANGE IN THE OUTCOME OF THE WAR

After drawn-out talks among the Allies, it was decided to open a second front in Europe to try and bring Germany to its knees. The attack on 'Fortress Europe' began on 6 June 1944 with the Normandy landings of more than 600,000 men – the largest armada ever assembled – under the command of the American General Dwight Eisenhower. The Allies could count on superiority in numbers and greater effectiveness, since many German troops were weary after long stints on other fronts. Allied success was also helped by the surprise factor, as well as by tactical wavering from the German command, partly caused by an elaborate decoy operation. The Allies' advance was swift: Paris was liberated on 25 August, Brussels on 3 September, and on 21 October the Allies reached the first major city in Germany – Aachen.

The tide was turning rapidly on the other fronts, too. In September 1943, after the Allies had landed in Sicily and a *coup d'état* had taken place against Mussolini, Italy signed the armistice.

On the Eastern Front, the last German offensive had failed and the Red Army continued its westward march to reach eastern Prussia in October. With Italy now out of the war, the second half of 1944 saw a progressive erosion of the alliances around Germany: Finland, Bulgaria and Rumania fell one after the other.

AMERICAN MARINES LANDING IN NORMANDY In one of Robert Capa's most memorable pictures, taken during the landings on 'Omaha Beach' on 6 June 1944, marines wade towards the beach under murderous German machine-gun fire. The 1st American infantry division suffered terrible losses in that sector. © Robert Capa/Magnum Photos

A V2 on the Launch Ramp
Called the 'flying bomb', it was used by the Germans to bomb English cities towards the end of the war.

The Allied Conferences

During the war, the Allies organized a series of conferences to discuss the outlines of what shape post-war Europe would take. The common aim was to defeat Germany and then punish it to stop it from unleashing yet another war. At Casablanca in January 1943, the American President Franklin Delano Roosevelt agreed with Winston Churchill on the demand for Germany's 'unconditional surrender'.

In Teheran the following November, Roosevelt, Stalin and Churchill decided to move the Polish border to the River Oder and assigned the northern part of eastern Prussia to the Soviet Union. Germany was not yet the main bone of contention between the big three, but there were still some major disagreements. Roosevelt wanted the substantial dismemberment of Germany into six independent regions, thus depriving it of its foundation of power – Prussian supremacy, territorial unity and economic strength. The British suggested a tripartite military occupation of the whole of Germany, total de-Nazification and demilitarization, and severe war reparations. Soon afterwards, the demarcation lines were drawn for the future occupation sectors in Germany.

In February 1945, the United States, Britain and the

German Driver Killed by Partisans in a Dutch City
In Italy, France, Yugoslavia and Greece, the war of liberation against their German occupiers was fought by the masses.

THE RESISTANCE AGAINST NAZISM

There was never an armed resistance movement organized in Germany as there was in every country the Nazis occupied and which, despite profound national differences, always provided a significant military, political and ideological contribution to the Allied war effort. The internal front was increasingly split, although most Germans – pushed by the terrorist policies or seduced by propaganda – stayed passive until the war ended. The longer it went on and the more remote a rapid victory seemed, the more active opposition began to grow in various places. Those who opposed Hitler – and they came from many different political alignments – were neither in agreement on what their mission should accomplish nor what methods should be adopted. Many had a limited range of action, by and large at local level, and often they had no idea that other groups even existed. Those from the old political or trade union set-up opted for the tactic of struggle, preferring to use propaganda to penetrate the masses. Among these groups, the Communists were the most active. They became increasingly independent from the leaders of the movement in Moscow and distributed leaflets, engaged in sabotage and spread news about how the war was going. They were mostly organized in the big cities where they plugged in to an existing network of contacts; the networks of the most active were far-reaching. Most of them fell victim to the close monitoring system of the Gestapo. There were also forms of opposition among the young, who were ill-disposed to the strict monitoring of the *Hitlerjugend* and felt let down by the unfulfilled promise of renewal. Many took refuge in groups with no political connotation who simply wanted to highlight how the totalitarian aims of Nazism had failed. Among university students, the 'white rose' group of Munich, which operated between June 1942 and February 1943, was one of the best known and most active. The main leaders, the Scholl brothers, made Christianity- and humanitarian-based appeals, especially by pamphleteering. After the Stalingrad defeat, they called for open struggle against the regime. The explosion of the conflict and the disastrous way the war was progressing gave many conservatives a reason for distancing themselves from the regime. National-conservative resistance thus came into being, albeit with many diversified features and origins, with men who had never stood up against the regime, even in 1933. A long apprenticeship was needed to understand the criminal aspects of which the Nazi government were the intimate essence. In the national-conservative resistance, and in particular the groups that came together in the attempt on Hitler's life on 20 July 1944, there was scant debate on what direction future policy should follow; every hypothesis agreed that there was to be a 'revolution from on high'. The aim was to restructure the regime in a more conservative-authoritarian way, curb the political weight of the NSDAP and National Socialism – but not repeal other things the regime had introduced, such as the destruction of the organized workers' movement – and pursue the formation of the 'community of people', rearmament and the first steps of an expansionist policy.

'People's Tribunal' Passing Judgement on the Conspirators of 20 July 1944 (Above left)

Hans Scholl (Above right)

Mussolini Visiting the Rastenburg Headquarters and the Room Half-Destroyed by the Bomb

Churchill, Roosevelt and Stalin at Yalta
The conference held in the Russian city assured cooperation among the Allies up to the end of the war. Stalin wanted a divided Germany when the war ended and repeated that the USSR was determined to be the hegemonic power in central Europe.

Capture of German Snipers in Leipzig, 1945

(Below)

Soviet Union reached an agreement at Yalta on the zones of occupation of the Reich, on how Berlin would be divided, and on acknowledging France as the fourth occupying power. Stalin was the most intransigent on the issue of German war reparations because his country had suffered more from Nazi aggression than any other. Churchill and Roosevelt feared that they would have to foot the bill of supporting Germany and putting it back on its feet if their countries were made to pay too much. Soon after the Yalta meeting, Stalin declared his opposition to dividing Germany – he placed more importance on the issue of reparations than the other two, reparations that would only be feasible if the country stayed united. He also wanted joint control of the Ruhr, and in order to get at its resources he was willing to make substantial concessions. France opposed this motion and it soon became clear that coordinated management of the defeated country would be impossible; the Allies decided to put their political disagreements on hold until the common goal of defeating the Reich had been accomplished. At the end of the war, however, the need for common agreement at all costs failed, with national interests and ideological differences coming to the fore.

Defeat

As the Allies continued their advance towards the heart of Germany from both east and west, heavy bombing was razing German cities to the ground. Cologne, Dresden and Berlin suffered tens of thousands of deaths, with most housing reduced to rubble and the everyday lives of Germans punctuated by air-raid sirens. The more desperate the situation became, the more Goebbels waged his ideological battle, repeating his claim that the Reich would win in the end.

KILLED BY A SNIPER Robert Capa's photograph shows the body of an American soldier hit by a German sniper posted on a rooftop in Leipzig in April 1945. The desperate resistance put up against the Allied advance was often prompted by the no-surrender order that Hitler had also given to the very young recruits. © Robert Capa/Magnum Photos

THE NERO DECREE

When defeat appeared to be inevitable, Hitler issued a number of draconian orders from his bunker below the Chancellery to prevent total Allied victory. The 'Nero Decree' was issued on 19 March 1945: 'The struggle for the existence of our people compels us, even within the territory of the Reich, to exploit every means of weakening the fighting strength of our enemy, and hindering his further advance. Every opportunity must be taken of inflicting, directly or indirectly, the utmost lasting damage on the striking power of the enemy. It is a mistake to think that transport and communication facilities, industrial establishments and supply depots, which have not been destroyed, or have only been temporarily put out of action, can be used again for our own ends when the lost territory has been recovered. The enemy will leave us nothing but scorched earth when he withdraws, without paying the slightest regard to the population. I therefore order: all military transport, and communication, facilities, industrial establishments and supply depots, as well as anything else of value within Reich territory, which could in any way be used by the enemy immediately or within the foreseeable future for the prosecution of the war, will be destroyed.'

YOUNG GERMAN SOLDIERS MOVING TOWARDS PRISON CAMPS

The 'Nero Decree' issued by Hitler recalled the 'scorched earth' policy that the German armed forces had put into practice during their retreat from eastern Europe. When the Red Army was approaching Berlin, the only battalions the Reich could muster against it were the newly formed Deutscher Volkssturm (German People's Militia), which was composed of youths born in 1928.

RUSSIANS AND AMERICANS MEET ON THE BRIDGE
Soldiers from the two victorious powers shake hands on the bridge over the River Elbe.

SURRENDER OF THE THIRD REICH
9 May 1945: Field Marshal Wilhelm Keitel (pictured centre) before signing the unconditional surrender in the headquarters of the Soviet Marshal Georgij Zukov in Berlin. (Below)

While continuing to point to the Judeo-Bolshevik danger, propaganda was now covering other issues. Hitler was no longer being portrayed as the greatest military genius humankind had ever seen – Stalingrad had put paid to that – but as 'Atlas, carrying the weight of the world on his shoulders'; the German soldier became 'defender of civilization'. Even secret weapons became a *leitmotif* of the Füher's declarations. Shortly after the Normandy landings, the first V1 flying bombs were sent across the Channel to England, causing serious destruction, especially in the London area. However, Britain soon strengthened its anti-aircraft defences, and the V1 had no effect on the outcome of the war.

The attempt on Hitler's life by Colonel Claus von Stauffenberg on 20 July 1944 showed that a struggle had broken out within the Nazi power structure between those who wanted to continue fighting to the bitter end, and those who supported a *coup d'état* as the first step to breaking off hostilities. Most of the population, now on its knees, was looking forward to the end of the war. In the early months of 1945, the Allies reached the heart of Germany from both east and west, and in so doing discovered the extermination camps and the horrors of the Holocaust.

By April, not even the most loyal of the Führer's henchmen thought that the course of the war could be reversed. On 30 April, Hitler committed suicide, and in his will he appointed Admiral Karl Dönitz as his successor. On 7 May, Germany surrendered, bringing hostilities in Europe to a close.

The statistics of World War II were catastrophic: 13 million people were executed, including six million Jews, three million Soviet prisoners of war and two-and-a-half million Poles. Four million German soldiers and some 17 million Allied soldiers died. In total, over 50 million people lost their lives.

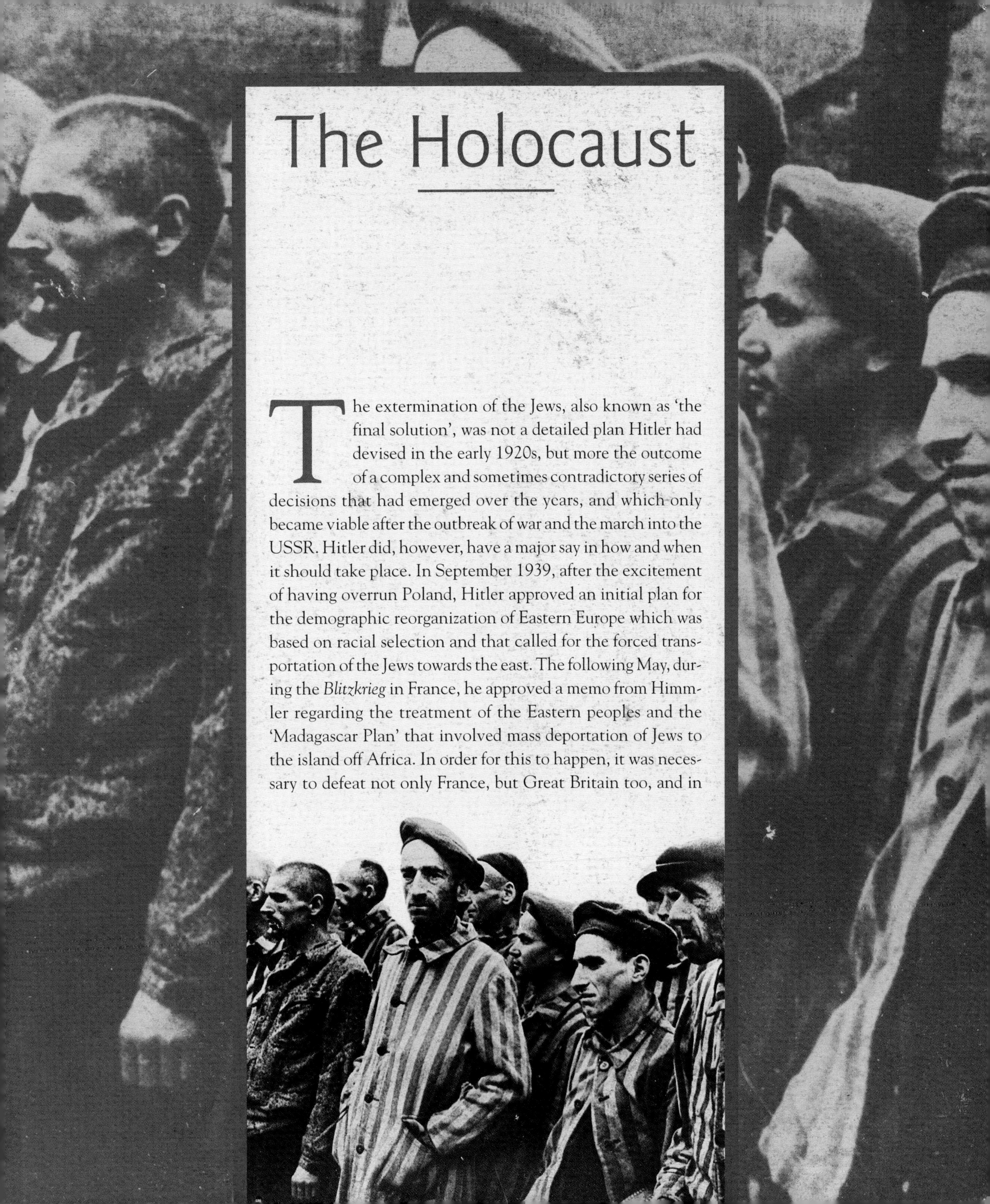

The Holocaust

The extermination of the Jews, also known as 'the final solution', was not a detailed plan Hitler had devised in the early 1920s, but more the outcome of a complex and sometimes contradictory series of decisions that had emerged over the years, and which only became viable after the outbreak of war and the march into the USSR. Hitler did, however, have a major say in how and when it should take place. In September 1939, after the excitement of having overrun Poland, Hitler approved an initial plan for the demographic reorganization of Eastern Europe which was based on racial selection and that called for the forced transportation of the Jews towards the east. The following May, during the *Blitzkrieg* in France, he approved a memo from Himmler regarding the treatment of the Eastern peoples and the 'Madagascar Plan' that involved mass deportation of Jews to the island off Africa. In order for this to happen, it was necessary to defeat not only France, but Great Britain too, and in

Shoes Belonging to Deportees in the Auschwitz Extermination Camp
(Page 160)

Jews in a Camp
(Page 161)

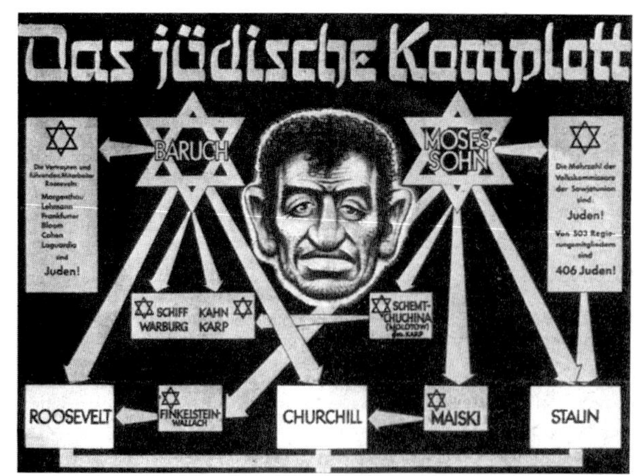

Jewish Conspiracy
German poster pointing to a link between the USA, the USSR and Great Britain.

Anti-Semitic Posters on Shops Owned by Jews
(Below)

mid-September 1940, it was clear that this was not going to happen in the short term. In July 1941, after the Nazi armies had penetrated deep into Soviet territory, Hitler approved a draft plan for the extermination of European Jews. Nazi racist policies started to become more radical as German military successes piled up, and it was only during the course of the war that they became as monstrous as they did.

During the Conference of Wannsee (20 January 1942), a number of guidelines concerning the final solution were drawn up, but it was decided not to carry them out. The head of the security police, Heydrich, convened the most representative echelons of the Reich and the general outlines of the operation were decided upon. The statistics regarding the number of European Jews to be exterminated were also prepared: 11 million, which included Jews who lived in countries allied to Germany.

The Jews in Germany

After the 'night of the broken glass', anti-Semitic persecution grew apace: firstly, Jews in large cities were grouped together, and secondly, they were kept separate from non-Jewish Germans. The former was the result of economic restrictions and was not organized systematically, whereas the latter was planned down to the smallest detail. In Germany and in the protectorates of Bohemia and Moravia, there were no ghettoes as in Poland and Russia, but similar living conditions were imposed.

The real quantum leap in anti-Semitic persecution came when non-Jewish Germans were obliged to break off social contacts with German Jews. There were fewer places made available for the Jews to live and they were evicted as soon as it became possible to move them elsewhere. In 1941, all the Jews were obliged to move to *Judenhäuser* (houses for

Drancy Internment Camp
The camp held French Jews and Jews from elsewhere who lived in France during the war.

Deportation From the Warsaw Ghetto
The Wehrmacht's racist war soon turned into a gargantuan operation of brutal demographic and social reorganization first carried out in Reich-occupied Poland. (Below)

Jews) that were run by the Jewish communities. Their daily movements were strictly regulated: in 1938, Jews had their driving licences revoked, and the following year they were forbidden to stay out after 8 pm. In 1941, they were forbidden to leave their town of residence, use public transport at rush hour, or have a telephone, and from 1942 they were totally forbidden to use public transport.

Special means of identification were introduced. In 1938, the passports of German Jews were marked with the letter J for *Jude* (Jew). From 1941, they had to wear a yellow star on their clothes to make them immediately identifiable to the police. Emigration, which had been encouraged up to 1939, was banned from autumn 1941, and this completed Jewish isolation from the remainder of the population. The next step, deportation, was only a matter of time.

The Ghettoes

Shortly after the Nazi attack on Poland of 21 September 1939, it was decided to set up ghettoes; every community had to have a *Judenrat* (Jewish council), who would be responsible for carrying out the orders of the Reich. The first major ghetto was established at Lodz in April 1940, the Warsaw community followed in October and many others were set up over the next few months. Although there was no overall directive, the issues faced were the same everywhere. The preparations were cloaked in great secrecy and the Jews were moved in without warning so as to prevent anyone escaping. Some Jewish communities were closed down within small cities that thus became city ghettoes. By the end of 1941, all the Jews in the occupied territories and in the governorate general of Poland were segregated. Now wholly cut off from the rest of the world, the ghetto had to solve all its internal

Cold-blooded Execution
An inhabitant of the occupied territory of Belarus before being killed by a German soldier.

The Uprising of the Warsaw Ghetto
The uprising began on 19 April 1943 and ended after desperate resistance by the armed Jewish militia on 16 May. More than 56,000 Jews died. What was left of the ghetto was razed to the ground by the Wehrmacht. (Below)

problems on its own. Contacts with abroad were severely restricted or forbidden. All Jews had to wear the yellow star and respect the curfew. It became impossible to purchase basic foodstuffs on the free market, and those available on the black market or through contraband were insufficient. Malnutrition, disease and death – especially through epidemics – spread rapidly, and 25 per cent of the Jewish population died before they could be deported to the extermination camps.

The ghettoes gave the *coup de grace* to the Jewish communities of Eastern Europe. Jewish companies were liquidated and the ghetto walls barred access to the factories and craftsmen's workshops that still existed. Jewish council members tried to solve these problems while carrying out the orders of the Germans, and the difficulty of being the intermediary between Jew and Nazi, victim and butcher, did not make their job easier.

The *Einsatzgruppen* and Mass Slaughter

The *Einsatzgruppen* were mobile units especially active in the military campaigns of Eastern Europe. First seen in 1938 during the occupation of Austria and as supporting units of the police secret service to the invading forces, they came into action during the invasion of Czechoslovakia and Poland to safeguard the security of the occupying forces' regime. In April 1941, after the attack on the USSR, new formations were established, each divided into four groups of some 3,000 men. These mobile units comprised members of the security police and security service, and had the basic task of killing political enemies and those deemed 'racially undesirable'. They could work both in the rearguard and also at the front. In order to reach as many cities as possible, the *Einsatzgruppen* followed the advance of the Wehrmacht, thus catching their victims before they had time to flee. To begin with, only adult males

Jews of Lodz Piled into a Cart
In this Polish city the Jews were permitted to work for the economy of the Reich before being deported to be exterminated.

Elderly Woman Wearing a Yellow Star
(Below left)

Pile of Rubble
All that was left of the old Jewish ghetto in Warsaw after the Germans decreed its destruction. (Below right)

were assassinated, but very soon the same fate awaited women, the elderly and children. The Wehrmacht gave much more than simple logistical support to these operations – they took an active part in handing Jews over to the *Einsatzgruppen*, they demanded to participate in mass executions and they shot hostages in reprisal for attacks against the occupying troops. From the second half of 1941, assassinations were organized using trucks with the exhaust fumes discharged inside them – a somewhat less brutal method for the executioners than the mass shootings from close range. During the German advance eastwards, some 500,000 people were exterminated.

Deportation

In November 1941, the final phase of the extermination began with the systematic deportation of the Jews from Germany. In October 1941, the Jews were told about the assembly points, rules of conduct and what belongings they should bring for what was described as a 'move to the eastern territories'. They were told to leave their homes with all the bills paid, and that all their assets had been requisitioned by the police with retroactive effect. The Jewish communities gave the Gestapo lists from which a selection was made, and since the number of deportees was more than the trains could carry,

French Edition of the *Protocols of the Elders of Zion* Published in Vichy in 1943
Nazi anti-Semitic propaganda made widespread use of the forgery the Tsarist police had carefully concocted in the early 20th century.

Jews in the Warsaw Ghetto
The inhuman living conditions its inhabitants were forced to live in soon turned the Warsaw ghetto into a breeding place of disease. (Below)

it was possible to apply for a postponement or exchange for what was thought would be a move to a labour camp in some undefined land to the east. In the second phase, when the death camps came into operation, these community and police lists were used to break into houses without warning. The deportations began from the Reich; Poland was next as the ghettos were progressively emptied.

The geographic scale of the 'final solution' was the most complex administrative issue facing the Nazis in their desire to exterminate the European Jews. The Poles and Russians were given no authority for managing this complex mechanism – no centralized power could operate that was not German. The Europeans of the north, west and south may not have been allies, but at least they had the potential to be, and in this 'semi-circular arc', the Germans gave instructions to central puppet organizations and made their demands known to the satellite governments. As the Polish ghettoes were emptying and massacres were being perpetrated in the east, the final solution was extended to Western Europe with the simultaneous launching of deportation programmes from France, Belgium, Holland and the Nordic countries. In March 1943, it was the turn of the Jews in Thessalonica, followed by those in the rest of Greece and then, in the following October, the Jews in Italy.

The Concentration Camps

The outbreak of war was a significant turning point in the complex concentration camp system. At that time there was a massive wave of arrests, and a decree of 20 September 1939 made it legal to kill prisoners who had committed serious crimes; this made deaths no longer merely attributable to indirect causes (disease, epidemics or malnutrition), but

YELLOW STAR
In many east European cities, the deportation of the Jews to the extermination camps was preceded by full-scale local nationalistic pogroms against the Jewish communities.

expressly authorized. There was a fall in the number of Germans being held and a rise in the number of foreigners and Jews detained. Up to 1941, the rise in arrests was gradual, in particular due to the arrival of detainees from occupied territories. In 1941, special units were created for Soviet prisoners. New camps including Auschwitz, Neungamme and Gross Rosen were built. In 1942, there was another turning point towards the decisive phase of the final solution – from this point on, the Jews became the absolute majority of detainees.

As early as 1938, the concentration camps had not only been for re-educating the enemies of the state but the economic interests of the SS had begun to have greater weight in decreeing how they were to be run. In the winter of 1941–42, using prisoners as a labour force became common, and over and above their function as detention centres, the camps turned into places of forced labour, with inhumane conditions and working regimes.

Then, in March 1942, the responsibility for the camps came under the economic administration of the SS, who turned the screw even tighter in the merciless exploitation of the labour force.

The concentration camps were organized in such a way that the structure was made an integral part of the repression mechanism. They were normally rectangular, with control towers at each corner to monitor all the detainees. The perimeters were made of barbed wire, and to emphasize the impossibility of escape, surveillance was concentrated along this line.

The gate represented total isolation from the outside world, underlined by the sadistic irony of the inscription at the entrance to Auschwitz: 'Work Makes Free'.

ANNE FRANK'S HOUSE
The young girl from Germany, obliged to seek refuge in Amsterdam, and whose story has become the symbol of the Holocaust bequeathed to us her *Diary*, a terrifying testimony of the atrocities committed by the Nazis. Anne Frank, together with her family, was deported to the camp at Bergen-Belsen, where she died of typhus.

ZYKLON B
Hydrocyanic acid fixed on silicon tablets and used to asphyxiate the deportees in the gas chambers.

REMAINS OF A CREMATORIUM OVEN AT BIRKENAU

AN AMERICAN SOLDIER LOOKING AT JEWISH CORPSES IN THE CAMP AT DACHAU
(Below)

THE EXTERMINATION CAMPS

Between 1941 and 1942, the extermination camps of Sobibòr, Treblinka, Chelmo, Majdenek, Belzec and Auschwitz II (Birkenau) came into operation in occupied Poland expressly for the murder of deportees.

Here, two-and-a-half to three million people, mostly Jews, were put to death. The creation of extermination camps made the massacre no longer the consequence of savage brutality on the part of special units but the result of planned, scientifically premeditated, industrialized genocide. Extermination camps were not merely the extreme limit of segregation of a large part of society, which had already been put into practice with concentration camps and ghettoes; they demanded the direct or indirect participation and complicity of many component parts of the German state machine – as well as of German society and of the collaborators in occupied countries – in a planned operation of mass extermination.

When victims reached the extermination camps there was no selection – everyone was to be put to death immediately. The wait was at most a few hours; then the victims were sent to the gas chambers, making them believe that this was just another transit point on their journey eastward. This cowardly expedient was carefully organized: garments had to be left outside the gas chamber and valuable possessions deposited in a special place. Everything was organized to make it easy to exploit the possessions of those that were sent to their deaths.

Only those involved in moving the bodies from the gas chambers to the ovens or the common graves to hide the evidence of what was happening were allowed a longer lease of life.

AUSCHWITZ: THE SYMBOL OF THE HOLOCAUST

Auschwitz was the biggest Nazi concentration and extermination camp, and is now seen as a symbol of the Holocaust. Some of the most noteworthy testimonies on deportation – including Primo Levi's *If This is a Man* – were written by people imprisoned there. The first nucleus of the camp, Auschwitz I, was completed in 1940 from a Polish artillery barracks. The prisoners were put to forced agricultural labour and to work in factories owned by the SS. In 1943, it contained 20,000 people; resistance movement fighters, Polish hostages and the intelligentsia from a variety of countries were put to death there. The Auschwitz II camp, known as Birkenau and three kilometres from Auschwitz I, was opened between the end of 1942 and early 1943; it was continually being added to until it covered some 2,000sq km. It was divided into various sub-camps – a camp for the Roma gypsies (the only people held according to family groups) and a camp for those deported from Theresienstadt. Auschwitz III, near Monowitz, was built for the chemical company IG Farben at the end of 1941 to use forced labour to help produce synthetic materials. All the 40 or so camps in upper Silesia came under the jurisdiction of Auschwitz III. In September 1941, the programme of gassings using Zyklon B commenced in a cell in block II of Auschwitz I. It was found to be too small, however, and so a gas chamber was built in the crematorium and used mainly to kill Soviet prisoners of war and small groups of Jews; it continued functioning until the end of 1942. In early 1942, the 'final solution' became so massive an operation that larger gas chambers were built at Birkenau which were used to murder the Jews from all the lands annexed to and occupied by the Reich.

On their arrival at Auschwitz, the deportees were divided as soon as they alighted from the trains: everyone deemed to be unfit for work – children and the elderly – were sent to the ovens immediately.

The others were saved, only to be killed later by the excesses of the work regime or the atrocious sanitary conditions. By order of Himmler, the gas chambers began to be dismantled at the end of 1944; the last was pulled down in January 1945, a few days before the Soviet troops arrived.

Two million men, women and children were murdered at Auschwitz.

JEWS AWAITING DEPORTATION TO THE EXTERMINATION CAMPS
News about the Nazi extermination programme began to circulate in early 1942. The Papal Nuncio in Bratislava passed information to the Vatican, the World Jewish Congress in Geneva discussed it, and information was also disseminated by a member of the Polish parliament in exile and picked up by the major American newspapers. It was not, however, enough to halt the Nazi industry of death. (Below)

The statistics of the genocide of the Jews in Europe

Country		Number	Country		Number
Poland	up to	3,000,000	Yugoslavia	more than	60,000
USSR	more than	800,000	Greece	more than	60,000
Rumania		400,000	Austria	more than	60,000
Czechoslovakia		260,000	Belgium		24,000
Hungary	more than	180,000	Italy (including Rhodes)		8000
Lithuania	more than	130,000	Estonia		2000
Germany	more than	150,000	Norway	fewer than	1000
Netherlands	more than	100,000	Luxemburg	fewer than	1000
France		83,000	Gdansk	fewer than	1000
Latvia		80,000	TOTAL	more than	5,000,000

EUTHANASIA AND EXTERMINATION OF THE ROMA

In April 1940, Hitler decreed that Operation T4 would begin, namely the euthanasia of the mentally ill and the handicapped; this was the first chapter of Nazi genocide. The ideology, the procedure of its decision and its techniques all link euthanasia to the final solution; all the victims were sacrificed in the name of Nazi biological racism. Sterilization and euthanasia were used to maintain the purity of the 'community of people', while extermination of the Jews – although itself seen as a process of racial purification – was essentially a fight against an enemy who was perceived as a threat to the survival of Germany and the Aryan race. The death centres of euthanasia, set in far-off places, had procedures aimed at concealing from the victims the tragic fate that awaited them: they were registered, given a medical 'examination', then sent into a gas chamber in a similar way to the victims of the extermination camps. More than 100,000 people were killed in this fashion.

The success of the euthanasia operation convinced the regime that mass murder was possible both because there were people willing to carry it out and also because most Germans chose to remain silent and did not stand in the way of what was happening.

The extermination of the Roma (gypsies) followed a path similar to that of the final solution; here, too, the war was a turning point in the persecution. On 2 September 1939, Roma nomadism in the Reich was outlawed and a month later the Roma were forbidden to leave their homes. Deportation to the concentration camps began in May 1940, and in 1941 they were the victims of the homicidal fury of the *Einsatzgruppen* on the Eastern Front. An order by Himmler

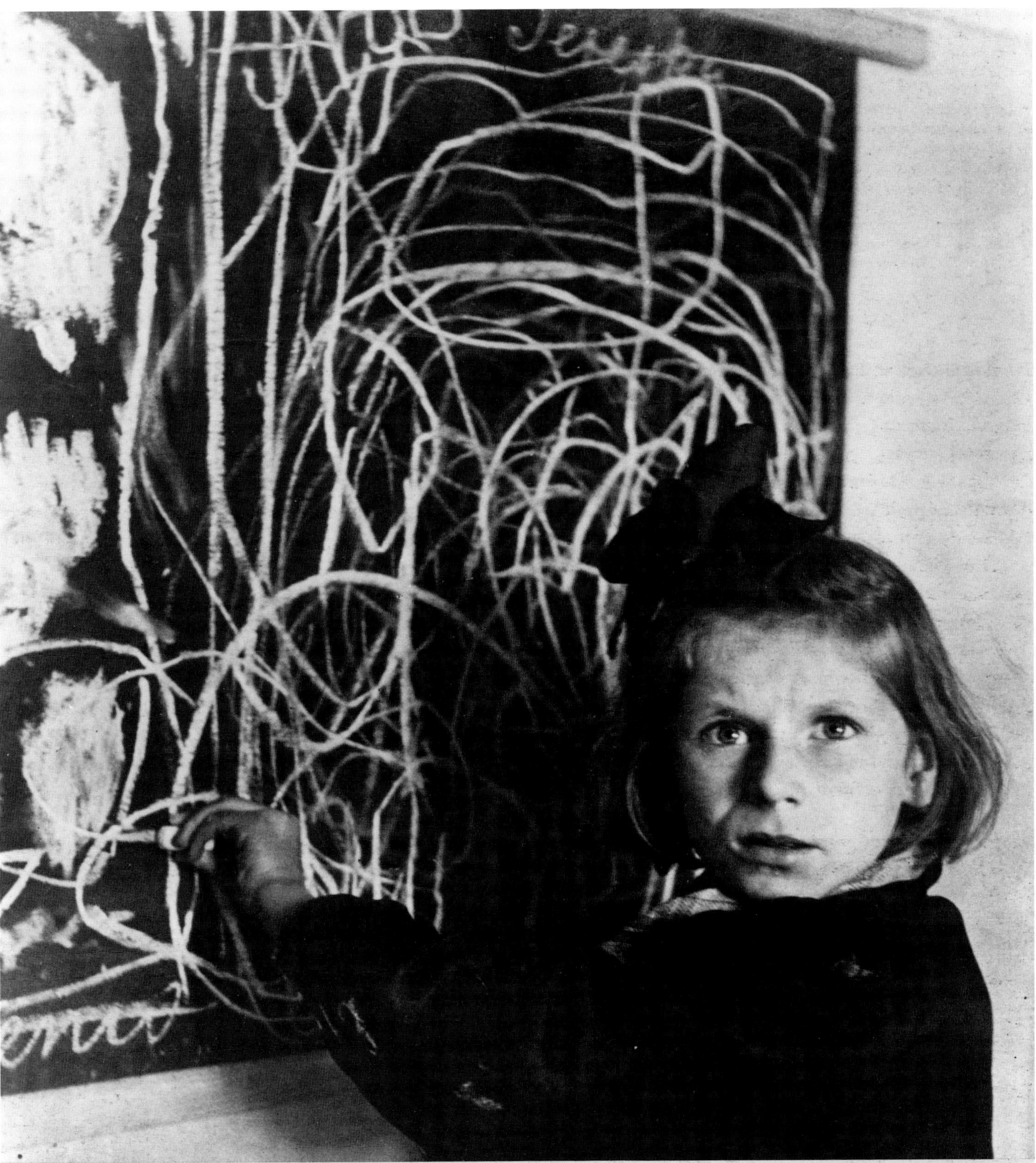

THERESA'S HOUSE When asked to draw a house, Theresa, a little Polish girl who had spent two years in a camp, responded with this testimonial of her psychological state after the extreme trauma she had lived through. The marks she drew on the blackboard were all she could draw of the inextricable tangle of lines of the barbed wire. © David Seymour/Magnum Photos

RUSSIAN PRISONERS
Between five and six million Red Army soldiers fell into German hands during the war. Of these, more than three million died of hardship, disease, forced labour and the inhuman treatment they were subjected to.

WOMEN IN A FORCED LABOUR CAMP
On their arrival in the forced labour camp, pregnant women were forced to have an abortion. (Below)

dated 12 December 1942 marked the final stage of the extermination. Exact numbers are difficult to calculate, but it is estimated that almost half a million Roma were killed in the Nazi death centres.

THE PRISONERS OF THE REICH

Prisoners were classified according to race and place of origin, namely where they stood in the Nazi race hierarchy. A coloured triangle on a uniform made everyone's status visible. One of the reasons for this subdivision was to stress the differences between the victims so as to make any kind of solidarity virtually impossible. It mattered little to the prisoners whether this system of classification responded to real differences or previous stereotypes; they took them on board and reciprocal differences were heightened. The Babel of languages made it even more difficult for contact to be made except among same-nationals. There were some exceptions, such as the Jehovah's Witnesses or the Spanish republicans. In the crowd, crushed together, each was stealing the place of his neighbour – one was never alone, but neither was one together with others. Forced cohabitation made any kind of social independence impossible; fraternizing was very rare and was often motivated by the need for survival such as for bartering food or primary necessities.

On their arrival, the victims were inducted immediately and violently into this new system, shorn and forced to wear a uniform, deprived of their individuality and reduced to a number, branded with a red-hot iron on their arm to emphasize the total eradication of their past and the beginning of the process of annihilation.

The separation between prisoner and camp staff, victim and butcher was carefully arranged so as not to be too clear

ADOLF EICHMANN: THE BUREAUCRAT OF EXTERMINATION

Eichmann was born in 1906, and after breaking off his engineering studies he decided on a career in sales. He joined the Austrian NSDAP and the SS in 1932, then moved to Germany, where in 1934 he became responsible for the Jewish question in the security service office in Berlin. He enthusiastically took charge of the plan to send the Jews east, and in 1937 travelled east in person to ascertain what real potential existed for such a plan to take place. After the *Anschluss* in 1938, he directed the organization in Vienna that managed Jewish emigration, and in October that same year he ran the central office of emigration in Berlin, providing him with extensive experience of expelling and deporting Jews. The following December, he rose to head Section IV B4 (questions regarding the evacuation of the Jews) in the Central Office for National Security and thus became the person most responsible for the deportation of Jews in occupied Europe. In March 1944, Eichmann was sent to Hungary, where he organized the deportation of Hungarian Jews to Auschwitz. When the war ended, he hid in Germany until 1950, then moved to Buenos Aires where he lived under the name of Ricardo Klement. Discovered by the Israeli secret service, he was taken to Jerusalem and placed on trial. During the hearings he declared that he had been a very small wheel and a simple executor of the orders he had received from his superiors in the complex machinery of extermination. He was hanged in 1962.

Wearing the Uniform of the SS, and the Accused at his trial in Jerusalem

THE EXTERMINATION: WHO KNEW?

The silence of the many who came to know about the genocide but did nothing was one of the factors that allowed the Nazi extermination machine to carry on for as long as it did. The automatism with which the machinery of death functioned, and the bureaucratic normalcy of the staff who made it work, were fundamental to this. However, the tradition of anti-Semitism, especially in Germany, dulled conscience and inhibition and fostered indifference in many even before the extermination had begun. Although shrouded in secrecy and carried out with great discreetness, the destruction of the Jews was too complex and extended an operation for news about it not to leak out. The spread of information about it by those who managed to escape, or the thousands of other ways that the news got through – such as, for example the testimony of the Germans themselves – were sufficient to provide an idea of the fate set aside for the Jews. The seriousness of what was going on in the heart of Europe was known quite early on. Envoys from the Polish government in exile were spreading news about extermination camps as early as the winter of 1942. A British propaganda pamphlet, presumably from early 1943, reads: 'Thanks to Germany, Poland has become the slaughterhouse where Jews not only from Poland but from all over Europe are being rounded up and massacred.'

Both the Allied and the collaborationist governments were informed of what was happening. In December 1942, the Allies condemned the policy of extermination of the Jews and promised sanctions against such crimes, but at that point defeating Germany and ending the war took priority over everything else, even the lives of millions of human beings. The Vatican was informed; through ecclesiastical channels news was coming through from every country. The anti-Semitic tradition of a large part of the Roman Catholic Church was certainly one of the factors behind its reticence, insensitivity and complicity. The Church certainly spared no effort in assisting the persecuted, but it fell short of an explicit condemnation of the crimes. The heads of the International Red Cross were informed even though their capacity for intervention became limited, besides which the deportation of the Jews presented it with issues that went well above and beyond its traditional scope.

INSIDE THE COURTHOUSE AT NUREMBERG

The Corpses of Camp Detainees Abandoned on a Railway Wagon

Liberating the camp at Dachau (Below)

and rigid. A complex hierarchical scale was devised based on each person's tasks and on forms of delegation of responsibility to auxiliary groups of internees who, in exchange for better food, were tied to the camp staff by complete loyalty and who fought to defend their positions from rival attack. This was one of the most perverse aspects of the Nazi system of domination – victims were transformed into accomplices.

Forced to live in inhuman conditions, many deportees to the camps soon lost all hope of survival, and were incapable of imagining any prospects for improvement. Many fell prey to the irreversible state of *Muselman* (one who gives up his soul to God): nothing more than human larvae, with no will to live and only death in their eyes.

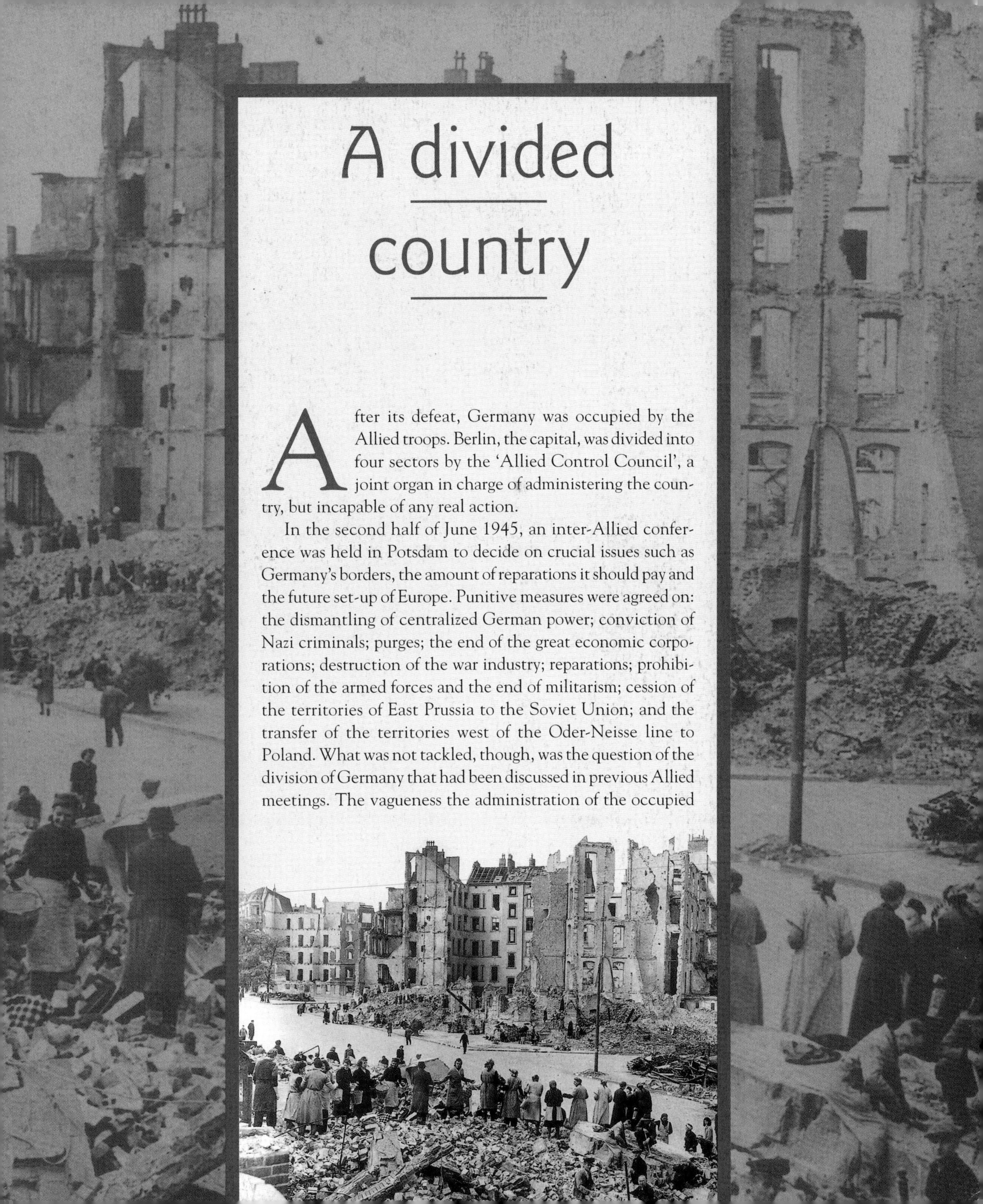

A divided country

After its defeat, Germany was occupied by the Allied troops. Berlin, the capital, was divided into four sectors by the 'Allied Control Council', a joint organ in charge of administering the country, but incapable of any real action.

In the second half of June 1945, an inter-Allied conference was held in Potsdam to decide on crucial issues such as Germany's borders, the amount of reparations it should pay and the future set-up of Europe. Punitive measures were agreed on: the dismantling of centralized German power; conviction of Nazi criminals; purges; the end of the great economic corporations; destruction of the war industry; reparations; prohibition of the armed forces and the end of militarism; cession of the territories of East Prussia to the Soviet Union; and the transfer of the territories west of the Oder-Neisse line to Poland. What was not tackled, though, was the question of the division of Germany that had been discussed in previous Allied meetings. The vagueness the administration of the occupied

AMERICAN SOLDIERS TAKING SNAPSHOTS IN NUREMBERG STADIUM
© Robert Capa/Magnum Photos
(Page 176)

BERLIN: A PILE OF RUBBLE
(Page 177)

ALLIED PRISONER OF WAR CAMP IN GERMANY

THE VICTORS AT THE POTSDAM CONFERENCE (Below)

zones had to deal with in actual political, economic and social measures was a contributing factor to the mood of incomprehension, which grew into division as the country increasingly became an arena in which the different hopes and desires of the two blocs was played out.

The most striking contradiction that emerged at Potsdam concerned reparations. It was decided that, despite the division of Germany into zones, reparations would be handled as though the nation was a single state. Each power was to receive war reparations from its own occupied zone, with an extra quota for the Soviet Union due to the heavier material damage it had suffered during the war.

POSTWAR GERMANY

The massive air bombardment inflicted by the Allies had destroyed many German cities, with the result that roughly seven million people were left homeless. Whereas industrial capacity was still largely intact, especially in the Soviet occupied zone, the transport system had been severely damaged.

Hunger was the most serious problem: in the course of the unusually long, cold winter of 1946–47, the harvest was destroyed by frost, and stockpiles were used up at the same time as energy supplies were beginning to run out. In 1939, the daily intake for the average German was 3,000 calories; ten years later it had fallen to just over 1,000. The black market became so widespread that the Allies were powerless to stop it. The situation was made even worse by the enormous influx of refugees from Eastern Europe – many were fleeing from Soviet troops or were being forced out of Poland and Czechoslovakia, countries that were implementing a policy of German expulsion. In each of the zones occupied by the British, Americans and Soviets, the population grew by roughly three million, creating problems of provisions, housing and jobs. Crime and infectious diseases like tuberculosis

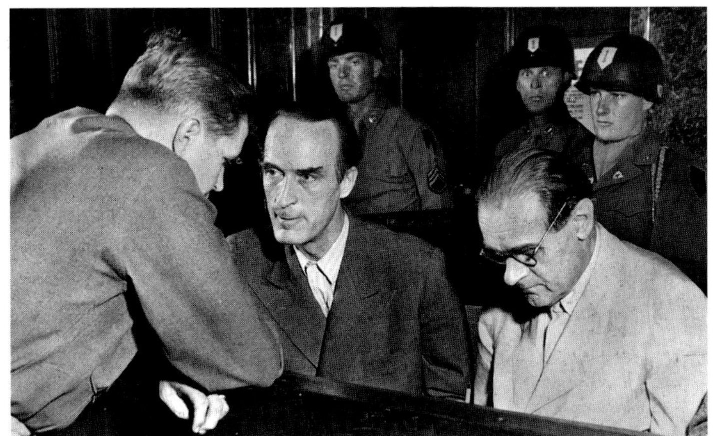

The Krupps Before the Court
A member of the family of steel magnates (pictured centre) on trial in an American tribunal after the war.

The Defendants Stand in the Courtroom of the Nuremberg Tribunal
(Below)

and typhus were widespread. Following the decisions taken at Potsdam, key economic and industrial sectors were dismantled, with consequences that were more serious psychologically than financially. Indeed, most Germans saw these measures as unjust punishment for a past that they did not feel responsible for as individuals. Instead of reflecting on the reasons for Nazism and its heritage, most Germans tended to avoid politics completely, closing themselves off into their own private worlds.

The Trials

In a joint statement issued in Moscow in November 1943, the Allies made it known that they intended to punish those who were responsible for war crimes. An international court comprising French, English, American and Soviet lawyers and judges put 24 defendants they considered chiefly responsible for Nazi policies on trial in Nuremberg. In the years that followed, there were many more trials under the jurisdiction of the separate occupying forces. The Americans held another 12 at Nuremberg, which were concluded in mid-1949, and during which 184 individuals were brought to justice. The trials, covering distinct aspects of Nazi policies – rearmament, the war in the Balkans, diplomacy and violation of international agreements – played a highly significant role in shedding light on the complex power structure of the Nazi regime, those responsible and their accomplices. The élite members of the regime were brought to justice, from Gauleiters to secretaries of state, from generals to heads of the SS. Officials responsible for Nazi policies in occupied countries during World War II were tried in other countries such as Holland, Italy, Poland and Czechoslovakia. But it was not until the 1960s that German courts also started to deal with crimes that were committed during the Nazi regime. Some of the most important trials concerned the administration

NUREMBERG

During the course of the trial held in Nuremberg from October 1945 to October 1946, the most important leaders of a state were put on trial and judged by a court of law for the first time in history. It had been repeatedly declared during the war that Nazi crimes were going to be punished, but in 1944 the Americans and the English were against the idea of a trial, preferring to simply execute the guilty. The stances that the separate Allies took *vis-à-vis* the defeated Nazis depended on the extent to which their countries had suffered during the war. Once the trial had been decided on, problems surfaced on how to single out defendants and their crimes. The Anglo-Americans were more interested in crimes against peace, and so wanted to try all the Nazi organizations that had collaborated in the war. On the other hand, the French and the Soviets, whose countries had suffered far more during the war, wanted to concentrate on war crimes. It was decided at Potsdam that the charges would be crimes against peace and conspiracy, war crimes, and crimes against humanity. The actual presence of the defendants at the trials depended wholly on chance – essentially, whether or not they had been captured by that stage. There were four members of the German army, a reflection of the American insistence on the war of aggression, but nobody from large-scale industry was charged. Whereas the Allies gave great ethical and political significance to the Nuremberg trial, the majority of Germans saw it simply as a vendetta by the conquering powers.

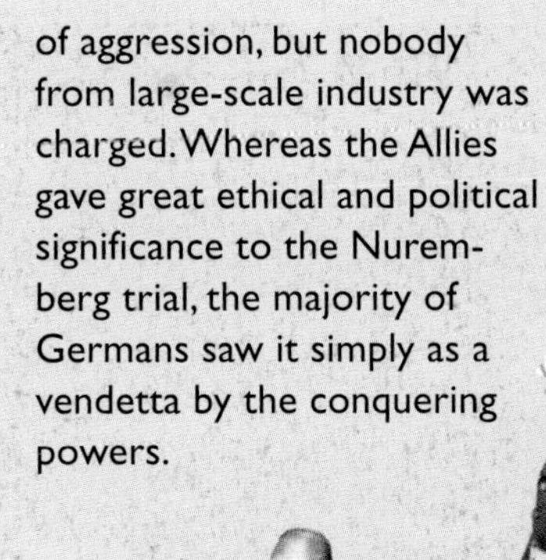

CHECKPOINT CHARLIE
American soldiers using binoculars to observe the checkpoint between the two sectors of Berlin. © René Burri/Magnum Photos

CHILDREN AT PLAY
The ghostly image of a square in Freiburg at the end of 1945. © Werner Bischof/Magnum Photos (Below)

of the concentration and death camps, such as the hearings on Auschwitz-Birkenau held in Frankfurt and those on Treblinka in Düsseldorf.

Many Nazi criminals managed to cover their tracks or to escape abroad, often assisted by the Catholic and Protestant churches. The Jerusalem trial of Adolph Eichmann, one of the main characters behind the extermination of the Jews, allowed the horrific nature of the Holocaust to be heard in public for the first time. But as the opposition between the two blocs intensified, the Allied tribunals ceased, and many of the condemned criminals or exponents of the Nazi regime were granted amnesty.

The Allied Occupation and the Growth of Conflict

The contrasts between the three western zones on the one hand and the Soviet one on the other grew sharper in the months following the end of the war, not only with regard to German issues, but also as a reflection of the general struggle for control of the international balance of power. In no other place did the Cold War have consequences as deep and immediate as it did in Germany, even if the board on which it was being played out was massive. In Turkey, Greece and Iran there was discord over territory between the Soviets and the Anglo-Americans, and this was to be the prelude to the clash of interests between the Soviet bloc and the Western powers that would cover the entire globe.

In July 1946, the United States proposed the economic unification of the four occupied zones to

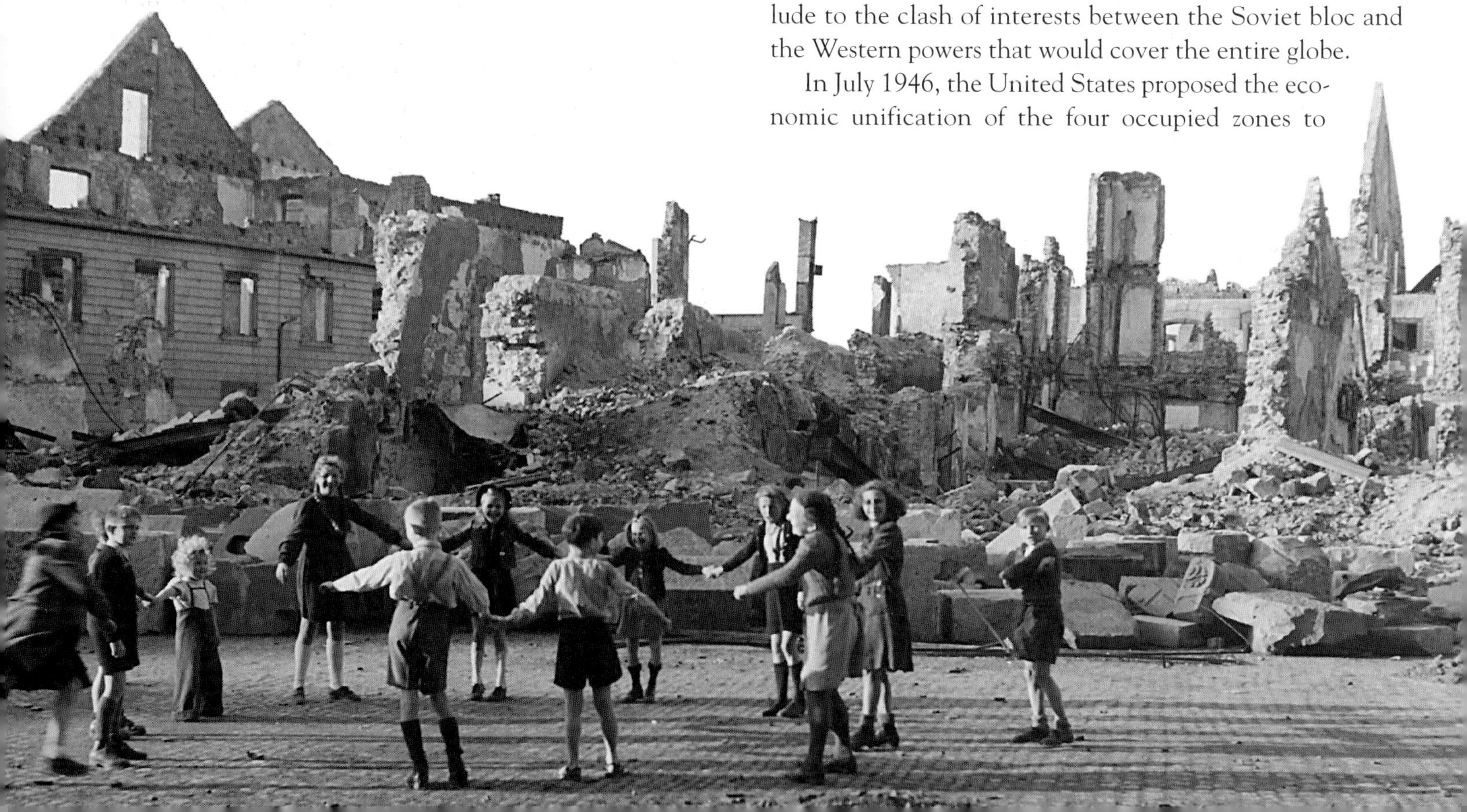

Full Speed Ahead For the Marshall Plan
In this poster, a lorry loaded with American aid crosses the German customs line. The European Recovery Program, better known as the Marshall Plan, was vital for the economic recovery of Europe and strengthened support for the new democratic governments.

improve the provisioning of the population, but the Soviet Union rejected the idea. At that point, Washington decided to speed up unification of the western zones, and on 1 January 1947 the economically unified 'Bi-zone' came into being, uniting the American and the British zones; on 8 April, it was joined by the French zone, thereby creating the 'Tri-zone'. The programme of aid based on the supply of credit, food and raw materials promoted by the US Secretary of State George Marshall played a highly significant role in the reconstruction of the German zones in Western hands. The USSR, by contrast, refused to take part in this programme, which it considered to be the first step towards total American political control. In June 1948, monetary reform was introduced in the 'Tri-zone' (the launch of the Deutsche Mark) in order to tap into the aid offered by the Marshall Plan. The Eastern zone responded with its own monetary reform, with which it intended to cover the whole of Berlin. On 18 June 1949, the tension turned into open hostility: the USSR blockaded all access roads to Berlin in an attempt to force the Allies to abandon the city. The Allies then responded with the greatest airlift in history: in just under a year the Americans made over 200,000 flights over the city, dropping two million tons of supplies for the population. The Cold War had now begun in earnest, and Berlin became the symbol of the struggle between the two blocs.

The Two Germanies

The Berlin blockade convinced the Allies to speed up plans for the political unification of the 'Tri-zone'; civilian powers were handed over to a German government, thereby creating the Federal Republic. In September 1949, the Conservatives won the elections, and Konrad Adenauer was appointed Chancellor. Burgomaster of Cologne during the Weimar Republic, he had been removed when the Nazis

Military Parade in the DDR
Parade of a division of the Nationale Volksarmee.
The creation of a national army in East Germany meant the country entered the political-military alliance of the Warsaw Pact, established in May 1955.

Watchtower Along the Berlin Wall
To prevent the flow of Germans from the East towards the Federal Republic, the military authorities closed the remaining passages between the two sectors of Berlin. There followed the building of the wall, in blocks of pressed concrete, which a DDR statement defined as 'the anti-Fascist defence wall'.

Tourists on the Border of the French Zone of the City
(Below)

came to power, and was therefore not tainted by involvement with the regime. The government he formed was still under tutelage of the Allies, who kept control not only of the Ruhr region but also of foreign politics and commerce, as well as all military affairs.

The Soviets kept a firm grip on the eastern zone, nationalizing banks and heavy industry. The great landholdings were confiscated without any indemnity. Some industries were transferred to the USSR as part of the reparations owed; others were managed directly by the Soviets and were exploited for the country, while still others provided the basis for the economic reconstruction of East Germany. One month after the foundation of the Federal Republic, in October 1949, the Democratic Republic was born. Kept under tight military control by the Soviet occupying army, East Germany developed under Soviet ideology, and for many years its economy suffered the effects of having to pay reparations.

As far as the political sphere was concerned, Moscow kept the situation under strict control, and the key positions of the administration that were left for Germans were given to Communists. The political parties were unified into one 'anti-Fascist bloc'; this was followed in 1946 by the fusion of the Communist and Social Democrat parties to form the SED (Socialist Unity Party), which took over the leadership of the country. In a short time, other political forces were disbanded, while the weight of the Social Democrats within the SED progressively diminished.

KONRAD ADENAUER
The architect of German reconstruction, in the course of Adenauer's long period as Chancellor he was also one of the promoters of European unity.

THE GERMAN FEDERAL REPUBLIC

Adenauer remained in power until 1963. His government, which could count on the substantial parliamentary majority of the Christian Democrat Union (CDU), was in close alliance with the United States, and its moderate political and social stance coincided exactly with the interests of large-scale capitalism. These postwar years witnessed spectacular economic growth in the German Federal Republic: intense working hours, considerable aid coming from America and a light burden of reparations all made for an extremely rapid recovery – between 1950 and 1963, the industrial production index leaped from 100 to 293.

The 'economic miracle' of these years brought domestic stability, but for many people the economic well-being made Adenauer's strict authoritarianism increasingly difficult to live with. Although he had restored federal Germany to a position of prestige in Europe and had made it the strongest nation against the Communist world, Adenauer's politics were deeply conservative.

The beginning of the 1960s saw the end of the most acute phase of the Cold War. In the 1961 elections, the CDU lost its absolute majority and Adenauer, representative of an era that was drawing to a close, left the post of Chancellor in 1963. The economic surge of the preceding years began to weaken; the voice of the opposition was growing stronger, and from 1964 on prices rose constantly. There was growing unrest, particularly among the nation's youth, with the lack of political renewal and in Germany, as in other European countries, 1968 saw the birth of a strong student movement. Meanwhile, the weight of the Social Democrat Party (SPD) had been growing, and in 1969 Willy Brandt became Chancellor. His politics were marked by a search for improved relations with East Germany (*Ostpolitik*) and by the resolution to 'dare for greater democracy'.

KNEELING BEFORE THE MONUMENT TO THE VICTIMS OF THE HOLOCAUST
The tragedy of the Holocaust was one of the thorniest problems in German-Polish relations. Here, in a gesture of enormous political and moral significance, German Chancellor Willy Brandt pays homage to the victims of the Warsaw ghetto in 1970.

ERICH HONECKER
Becoming successor to Walter Ulbricht as head of the SED in 1971, Honecker initiated a more open policy towards Bonn. Under his leadership, the DDR confirmed its position as the most highly industrialized country in the 'socialist camp'.

THE GERMAN DEMOCRATIC REPUBLIC (DDR)

The DDR's propaganda concerning the creation of a socialist state gave it a strongly idealistic thrust, but its economic revival was not immediately forthcoming, and its social and political life rigidly followed the Soviet model. East Germany was committed to a massive programme of reconstruction which resulted in a very low standard of living for most people. The SED controlled state and society, as well as the economy. The Minister for State Security, created in 1950, delved deep into society to prevent all forms of opposition. Public life was increasingly militarized and the cult of the state and of Communism was evident in every area of cultural society. The standard of living and the quality of goods were far inferior to those in West Germany, even though East Germany's economy was the healthiest of all the countries in the Communist bloc. In June 1953, the first workers' strike took place, initiated by overly rigid collectivization, low standards of living, and in protest at workers' long hours. The strike spread all over the country and was immediately put down by Soviet troops. At this point the SED was forced to recognize the limits of its power and just how dependent it was on the Soviet Union. The building of the Berlin Wall in 1961 tragically marked the need to keep a rigid separation between two worlds where one – the West – exerted a strong force over the other.

REUNIFICATION

One of the most significant effects of the collapse of Communism was the reunification of Germany. On the evening of 9 November 1989, the first holes appeared in the Berlin Wall. It marked the end of the separation between the two Germanies that had been the most obvious consequence of the defeat of the Nazi Reich and the era of the Cold War. The reasons for the fall of the Wall derived from a series of

RETHINKING NAZISM

In the aftermath of the war, the two Germanies were faced with similar problems: recovery from the material and moral consequences of the conflict and defeat; assessing how much guilt should attribute to Nazism and responding to the expectations of its victims and of the international community; and reintegrating a large number of ex-Nazis into postwar society. The history of the division of Germany is also the history of a divided memory of the Nazi past and of the opposition that had been organized against Hitler's regime. During the Cold War, both states tried to present themselves as the only possible legitimate Germany after Hitler, the Democratic Republic because it had torn up the economic roots of Nazism, the Federal Republic because it was anti-totalitarian. So the way each Germany saw its own history was doubly conditioned: firstly regarding Nazism, and then regarding the other Germany. In their attempt to gain international credibility, the two states also competed in reconstructing the past. In the Democratic Republic, de-Nazification was more radical than in the West, but anti-Fascism was imposed from on high and became state propaganda. The Comintern's 1935 definition of Fascism as extremist capitalism was still considered true, and having destroyed Nazism it was seen as final proof that a clean break had been made with the Nazi past. It was claimed that since only the Communist Party had carried out a full-fledged struggle against the regime, it was now the only legitimate force able to govern the country. What was lacking, however, was a reflection on the relationships of strength that had underpinned Nazism, the complicity and silence of the majority of the population, and what this implied as regards historical continuity and

Trabant
With its two-stroke, two-cylinder engine, the Trabant was the pride of the East German automobile industry, and it allowed many citizens of the DDR to enjoy the benefits of mass motorization.

complex changes that took place in the entire Communist bloc during the 1980s, and that started in the Soviet Union itself. There, much of the credit went to the leader of the Kremlin, Michail Gorbacëv, and his politics of reform. In East Germany, popular dissent had been growing from the outset of 1989. Many East Berliners did not return from holiday but applied for asylum in the West German embassies in Prague and Budapest; and there was a continuous flow of people through the passageways in the Wall. Newly formed opposition groups like the 'Neues Forum' were pressing for the extension of the reforms introduced in the Soviet Union to East Germany.

After the Wall fell, unification of the two states began to look increasingly likely. The East Germans fondly hoped that the Western model would be rapidly extended to the whole country. Feverish negotiations began between the United States and the Soviet Union, and on 3 October 1989, the President of the Federal Republic, Richard von Weizsäcker, officially announced unification. Although there may not have been any real alternative to this course of events, with hindsight it all happened too quickly. It ended up being more an 'annexation' of the eastern part of Germany by the western side, with nothing of the DDR's culture being conserved.

But decades of life in such different political systems could not be cancelled in one day, and soon there were many problems and mutual resentments to deal with. The electoral success of extreme right-wing parties in the former East Germany at the beginning of the 1990s, and the sharp rise in acts of racist and xenophobic violence within the region, suggest that there is still a long way to go before the true process of unification is complete.

the need for renewal to take place at all levels. In the Federal Republic, on the other hand, anti-Fascism was stigmatized as a Soviet ideology and so its historical legitimacy was rejected in favour of a blatant, deep-rooted and widespread anti-Communism. The past existed mainly in the many initiatives to speed up the de-Nazification process set in motion by the Allies. The Adenauer era was affected by a sort of amnesia in which the theory of the totalitarianism of others became part of the ideology of the state: Nazism and Communism were both considered opposite sides of the totalitarian coin, and the new German state, as an ally of the West, could now find its legitimacy and pay its debt for Nazism by combating the Communist threat. The Cold War implicitly rehabilitated the Nazi past. Ex-Nazis were seen as Germans who had merely done their duty as soldiers or state officials. The two decades following the war were dominated by a sense of collective innocence. This silence was not broken until the 1960s: the Eichmann trial in 1961 and the new spirit of the younger generation brought the Germans face to face with the past they had tried to ignore.

Skinheads
German neo-Nazi skinheads have been responsible for xenophobic and racist acts against foreigners living in Germany.

A SYMBOL OF THE 20TH CENTURY On 9 November 1989, the government of the DDR gave its citizens freedom to leave, and Berliners from both sectors of the city joined together in a spirit of popular festivity and celebration, the first real move towards reunification of the two Ge
manies. That day marked the culmination of the political upheaval that overturned the existing order in Eastern Europe during the course of that y

PLACES FOR REMEMBRANCE

The DDR placed great emphasis on adapting and conserving the concentration camps. In the early 1950s, the state took upon itself all the expenses of the restoration of the structures to keep them from falling into ruin, even if this was done for political motives. The memory of the camps was, in fact, kept alive unilaterally as a means of justifying – through the affirmation of the continuity of anti-Fascism – the Communist Party's role in a one-party state. In the presentation of the camps, in demonstrations held to commemorate anniversaries, and in museums, a privileged and even exclusive place was reserved to the martyrdom of Communists and German anti-Fascists, while both the international victims and the persecution of the Jews were forced into the background. In the Federal Republic, on the other hand, the places of remembrance never became patrimony of the state, and their organization and maintenance depended on the initiatives of private individuals and groups of victims, as evidenced in the case of Dachau. It has only been since the mid-1980s that the old concentration camps have started to be preserved not only as museums but also as research centres – often thanks to lengthy renovations that have enabled at least some of them to be recovered. Considerable encouragement has been given to the discussion of the ways of remembering the past through reunification which, along with more general issues deriving from the relation of the new nation state with Germany's past, has posed the immediate question of the acquisition of the DDR's state-run concentration camps for the reunified Germany. This has led to a wider reflection concerning both what is actually to be remembered (in consideration of new light shed by recent historical research) and the techniques of communication adopted today. Besides the numerous means used to recall the memory of places, facts and persons – including monuments, stones and simple place names – there has recently developed a strategy of setting up historical expositions and shows. The need to attend to the problem of remembrance has become more acute because of a growing awareness of the generation gap as a consequence of the breakdown of traditional channels of transmission, the death of witnesses and the continuity of the family memories that they guaranteed.

1918-1934

CHRONOLOGICAL TABLES

1918

9 November: Abdication of the Kaiser – the Weimar Republic is born.

1919

5 January: Foundation of the Deutsche Arbeiterpartei.

1920

24 February: The Deutsche Arbeiterpartei becomes the NSDAP and the 25-point programme is drawn up.

1923

January: French troops occupy the Ruhr.
8–9 November: Hitler's Munich Putsch.

1924

April: Hitler is sentenced to five years imprisonment.
December: Hitler is freed.

1925

February: The NSDAP is re-established.
April: Paul von Hindenburg is elected President of the Republic.

1930

January: The NSDAP wins its first regional government, in Thuringia.

1932

31 July: In the elections for the Reichstag, the NSDAP becomes the biggest party, with 37.4 per cent of the vote.

1933

30 January: Hitler appointed Chancellor by Hindenburg.
4 February: Decree 'For the Protection of the German People' limiting freedom of the press.
27 February: The Burning of the Reichstag.
28 February: Decree 'For the Protection of the People and the State' abolishing basic rights, authorizing preventative arrest and outlawing the Communist Party.
5 March: Elections for the Reichstag – the NSDAP wins 43.9 per cent of the vote.
13 March: Goebbels appointed Minister for Propaganda.
22 March: The concentration camp at Dachau is opened.
23 March: Measure granting full powers to the government becomes law.
1 April: Boycott of Jewish shops.
7 April: Measure providing for dismissal from state employment Jews and anyone considered politically suspect becomes law.
11 April: Hermann Göring appointed assistant representative of the Reich and President of the Prussian government.
21 April: Rudolf Hess appointed assistant to the Führer.
2 May: The trade unions are dissolved.
10 May: Burning of the books. Foundation of the German labour front.
19 May: The German labour front suppresses the right to collective bargaining.
17 June: Baldur von Schirach appointed head of the German Youth.
14 July: The law against re-establishing parties grants political monopoly to the NSDAP. Law for the prevention of hereditary diseases.
20 July: Concordat with the Vatican.
September: 'Victory Congress' in Nuremberg.
22 September: Law founding the House of Culture.
29 September: The Hereditary Farm Law.
14 October: Germany leaves the League of Nations.
12 November: One-party elections for the Reichstag: the NSDAP wins 92.2 per cent of the vote.
1 December: Law on the unity of state and party.

1934

27 February: Law regulating 'national work'
20 April: Heinrich Himmler appointed head of the Gestapo.
30 June: 'Night of the Long Knives'.
3 July: Hjalmar Schacht appointed Minister of the Economy.
1 August: Decree combining the posts of President and Chancellor of the Reich.
2 August: Paul von Hindenburg dies and Hitler becomes 'Führer and Chancellor'.
September: 'Congress of the Triumph of the Will' in Nuremberg. Schacht presents the 'New Plan'.

1935-1940
CHRONOLOGICAL TABLES

1935
13 January: Saar Referendum.
26 February: Law introducing the 'workbook' for control of the labour force.
16 March: Compulsory conscription reintroduced.
September: 'Liberty Congress' in Nuremberg, during which the 'Law in defence of the German blood and honour' and the 'Law on citizenship of the Reich' are promulgated.
18 october 'Law in defence of the hereditary biological purity of the German people'.
13 December: Establishment of the 'Lebensborne'.

1936
7 March: The Wehrmacht occupies the Rhineland, a demilitarized region.
29 March: Plebiscite on Hitler's policies: 99 per cent in favour.
17 June: Himmler named 'Reichsführer of the SS' and head of the German police in the Ministry of the Interior.
July: German military intervention in the Spanish Civil War.
August: Sachsenhausen concentration camp opened. Olympic Games held in Berlin.
September: 'The Congress of Honour' in Nuremberg, at which the four-year plan is launched
23 October: Proclamation of the Rome-Berlin Axis.
25 November: The anti-Comintern Pact is signed with Japan.
1 December: The *Hitlerjugend* become the State Youths.

1937
July: Buchenwald concentration camp is opened.
The show on 'degenerate art' is inaugurated in Munich.
5 November: Meeting of Hitler with military chiefs of staff, during which orders for the invasion of Austria and Czechoslovakia are issued.
26 November: Schacht resigns.

1938
4 February: Appointment of the Minister of War, Commander in Chief of the Army and Foreign Minister as part of preparation for war.
12 March: Austria annexed to the Reich.
April: Aryanization of Jewish-owned businesses begins.
29 and 30 September: Munich Conference: the Sudetenland is ceded to Germany.
1 October: German troops invade Czechoslovakia.
9 November: 'Night of the Broken Glass' and *pogrom* against the Jews.
8 December: Himmler issues a decree on census-taking and procedures for the identification of gypsies.

1939
15 March: Occupation of Czechoslovakia and the institution of the Protectorates of Bohemia and Moravia.
23 March: The Nazis invade the region of Memelburg/Klajpeda.
22 May: Signing of the 'Pact of Steel' with Italy.
23 August: Non-Aggression Pact between Germany and the Soviet Union.
27 August: Food rationing.
1 September: Germany attacks Poland: World War II begins.
October: Hitler drafts the authorization for the euthanasia programme.

1940
9 April: Germany invades Denmark and Norway.
10 May: Germany invades Holland, Belgium and France.
14 June: The Germans occupy Paris.
22 June: France signs an armistice with Germany.
10 July: The Battle of Britain begins.
27 September: Germany, Japan and Italy sign the Tripartite Pact.
October: Many Jewish ghettos created in Eastern Europe.
18 December: Directive No 21 issued by Hitler: preparation for the attack on the Soviet Union.

1941-1945

CHRONOLOGICAL TABLES

1941

11 February: Erwin Rommel arrives in Libya.

17–30 March: Hitler declares that the imminent Russian campaign will be a 'war of annihilation'.

6–8 April: Bulgarian, Germans and Italian troops invade Yugoslavia and Greece.

10 May: Martin Bormann appointed 'Head of the Party Chancellery'.

22 June: Germany invades the USSR.

14 July: Rosenberg appointed Minister for the occupied territories in the East.

1 September: Obligation for Jews to wear a yellow star.

1 October: Jews are banned from emigrating.

14 October: Deportation of German Jews to Eastern European ghettos.

6 December: Start of the Red Army counter-offensive.

7 December: Japanese attack on Pearl Harbor.

11 December: Germany declares war on the United States.

1942

20 January: Wannsee Conference – coordination of measures for the 'final solution of the Jewish problem'.

8 February: Albert Speer appointed Minister for Armament and War Production.

21 March: Fritz Sauckel appointed 'Plenipotentiary General for the Allocation of Labour'.

March: The first train-loads of German and Eastern European Jews leave for Auschwitz.

21 June: Rommel captures Tobruk.

June: The mass extermination of Jews gets under way at Auschwitz-Birkenau.

1 July: The First Battle of El-Alamein begins.

13 September: The Battle of Stalingrad begins.

24 October: The Second Battle of El-Alamein begins.

11 November: Germany occupies Vichy France.

1943

14–24 January: Allied Conference at Casablanca.

2 February: The Germans are defeated at Stalingrad.

18 February: Goebbels proclaims 'total war'.

13 May: The Axis powers defeated in North Africa.

26 June: Speer takes over full control of all war production.

8 September: Italy surrenders to the Allies.

9 September: The Germans occupy Rome and most of Italy.

12 September: The Germans free Mussolini.

13 October: Italy declares war on Germany.

28 November–1 December: Allied Conference in Tehran.

1944

20 February: Start of the Anglo-American air offensive against Germany.

6 June: Allied landing in Normandy.

20 July: Failed attempt on Hitler's life.

24 July: The Soviets liberate Majdanek death camp.

25 July: Goebbels named 'overall head for total war mobilization' and Himmler named supreme commander of the reserve army.

8 September: The first V2 missile hits England.

7 October: German withdrawal from Greece.

21 October: Aachen is the first German city to be occupied by American troops.

1 November: Himmler orders the extermination of Jews to be halted at Auschwitz-Birkenau.

1945

14 January: The Red Army invades East Prussia.

27 January: Soviet troops liberate Auschwitz-Birkenau.

19 March: The 'Order Nero' is issued.

30 April: Hitler commits suicide.

7 May: Alfred Jodl signs Germany's unconditional surrender to the Allies at Rheims.

17 July–2 August: Allied Conference at Potsdam.

Index of names

Photograph references

© Roger-Viollet/Contrasto 9, 10a/b, 11a, 12al/ar/b, 13c/b, 14a, 15b, 16, 17, 18al/b, 19, 20a, 21b, 23a/b, 24al, 26a/b, 27, 28, 29, 30al/b, 32, 33, 34b, 35a, 37b, 38b, 39b, 40br, 41b, 42b, 43b, 44al, 45, 46, 47a/br, 48, 49, 50a, 51a/b, 52b, 56a/b, 57a/bl/br, 60b, 61a/c/b, 62a/b, 63bl, 66a/bl, 67a, 69a, 71b, 72al/b, 74a/b, 75b, 76a, 77b, 78b, 79b, 82b, 83al/ar/b, 85al/b, 86a, 87b, 90al/ac/b, 91, 93a/b, 94al/ar/bl, 95a, 100ar/b, 103b, 105b, 110a/b, 113, 114b, 115a/bl/br, 116a/bl/br, 117a/b, 118a/b, 119a, 120a/b, 121, 123, 125al/b, 126b, 127, 128, 129, 131a/b, 132, 133, 134, 135b, 136a, 137b, 138a/b, 139a/br, 142b, 144b, 145c/bl 146b, 147a/b, 148bl/br, 149bl/br, 150a/b, 151a, 154a/b, 155b, 158, 162b, 163a, 172a, 173b, 175a, 178a, 179a/b, 183a

© Magnum/Contrasto 35bl, 37a, 39a, 41a, 44b, 50b, 84b, 107b, 119b, 122a/b, 124b, 130a, 135a, 136b, 137a, 140br, 141, 142a, 143, 144a, 146a, 148a, 150b, 152a, 153, 156b, 157, 159a/b, 160, 161, 163b, 164b, 165a/bl/br, 167b, 168ar/b, 169b, 170, 171, 172b, 173a, 175b, 176, 177, 178b, 180a/b, 181b, 182a, 184, 185a/b, 186

© Olympia/Publifoto 20b, 112, 182b, 183b

© Corbis/Contrasto 73

Where no specific indication is provided, the photograph is from the Giunti archives. As far as copyright is concerned, the publisher agrees to pay for all illustrations the sources of which were impossible to trace.

a (above), ac (above centre), ar (above right), al (above left), b (below), br (below right), bl (below left), c (centre page)